To my amazing wife, Melissa. Your unwavering support, love, and understanding further ignite my passion for the work that I do. Thank you for letting me follow my passion.

DIGITAL LEADERSHIP

Changing Paradigms for Changing Times

ERIC SHENINGER

Foreword by
YONG ZHAO

A Joint Publication

CORWIN
A SAGE Company

FOR INFORMATION

Corwin
A SAGE Company
2455 Teller Road
Thousand Oaks, California 91320
www.corwin.com

SAGE Ltd.
1 Oliver's Yard
55 City Road
London, EC1Y 1SP
United Kingdom

SAGE Pvt. Ltd.
B 1/I 1 Mohan Cooperative Industrial Area
Mathura Road, New Delhi 110 044
India

SAGE Publications Asia-Pacific Pte. Ltd.
3 Church Street
#10–04 Samsung Hub
Singapore 049483

Acquisitions Editor: Arnis Burvikovs
Associate Editor: Desirée A. Bartlett
Editorial Assistant: Ariel Price
Project Editor: Veronica Stapleton Hooper
Copy Editor: Lana Todorovic-Arndt
Typesetter: Hurix Systems Pvt. Ltd.
Proofreader: Talia Greenberg
Indexer: Karen Wiley
Cover Designer: Gail Buschman
Marketing Manager: Katie Stoddard

Printed in the United States of America.

Library of Congress Cataloging-in-Publication Data

Sheninger, Eric C.

Digital leadership : changing paradigms for changing times / Eric Sheninger.

pages cm.

Includes bibliographical references and index.

ISBN 978-1-4522-7661-8 (alk. paper)

1. Educational technology—Planning. 2. Educational leadership. 3. Education—Effect of technological innovations on. 4. School management and organization. 5. Education—Aims and objectives. I. Title.

LB1028.3.S4426 2014

371.33—dc23   2013034904

This book is printed on acid-free paper.

SUSTAINABLE FORESTRY INITIATIVE
Certified Chain of Custody
Promoting Sustainable Forestry
www.sfiprogram.org
SFI-01268

SFI label applies to text stock

14 15 16 17 18 10 9 8 7 6 5 4 3 2 1

Contents

Foreword

I deleted my Facebook account in June 2013, after having it for about two years and accumulating nearly 1,000 friends. Why? I hadn't found a reason to use it.

Finding reasons to use technology is one of the biggest challenges educators and education leaders face. Very few technologies are originally invented to serve an educational purpose. Quite often they are pushed into schools because, with hundreds of millions of potential users, the education sector represents a huge irresistible market. Technology then becomes a solution looking for a problem—in a subculture that frequently perceives the introduction of technology as a problem rather than a solution.

Don't get me wrong; I am not a Luddite. To the contrary, I have always believed in the potential of technology for improving education. I began writing software to teach English in 1985 and have designed a variety of technological products to support learning. I have also helped teachers and school leaders adopt technology and conducted research on the diffusion of technological innovation in schools. If anything, I can be called a technophile.

What I've learned is that the great potential of technology to improve education is not automatically realized. In fact, it is quite often not realized at all. The history of educational technology is filled with examples of unfulfilled promises and wasted investments that the technophiles don't want to talk about. From radio to TV, from multimedia to hypermedia, from films to the Internet, waves of modern information and communication technologies have promised to improve and transform education and have failed to do so. We can blame technology for its overhyped capacities, teachers for their unwillingness or inability to make good use of it, educational institutions for their stubborn resistance to change, or governments for their lack of sufficient investments. While the blame may appear justified, it doesn't accomplish anything. The constructive response is not to point fingers but to learn from mistakes.

One mistake has been an overzealous attitude toward technological innovation leading to the undervaluing of existing educational practices. Inspired by the great potential of technology, proponents wonder why everyone else doesn't "see the light" as they do. But the reality is that most educators feel fine with their own practices and are functioning satisfactorily in their work. The missing link is the thoughtful and meaningful application of technology to education. In other words, the potential of technology must be translated into meaningful solutions to educational problems. Only when such a translation occurs will the majority of educators find reasons to adopt it.

Eric Sheninger provides such a translation in this book. Drawing from his extensive experience as an education leader, Sheninger presents stories and examples of technology improving the effectiveness of schools. He frames technology as a solution to the "problem" of the school improvement mandate, from community building to communications, from professional growth to enhancing student learning, and from building a better brand to improving public engagement.

The aim of technological innovation is not only to enhance existing practices, but also to transform them. Humans develop technology to expand human capacities and occasionally to replace human labor in simple tasks. ATMs have largely replaced bank tellers, for example, as robots have replaced many workers on the assembly line. As a result of technological advancement, most industries in our society have undergone dramatic transformations and seek more complex human skills, knowledge, and abilities, which requires our students to develop different skills than their predecessors—skills that differentiate them from machines. Schools must adapt to help our children acquire these skills and knowledge.

Moreover, information and communication technologies have brought significant changes to the core business of schools. The teacher, for instance, has for a long time been the primary source of knowledge and agent of knowledge transmission for students. But that is no longer the case. Today's students theoretically have access to any information they desire and any expert they seek. This makes it necessary for teachers to seriously reconsider their role and their relationship with technology. If students can Google anything, why do they need teachers?

A redefinition of the role of teachers and schools has not yet emerged on a large scale. Sheninger pushes educators and education leaders to begin this work. More important, he uses meaningful examples to illustrate how we can begin the redefining journey.

I am grateful that Sheninger took the time to play with different technologies, to redefine his role as an educator and education leader, and to reflect on his experiences and put together such an excellent book. *Digital Leadership* provides a framework for leading educational transformation with technology.

Had I read this book earlier, I might have found my reason to stay with Facebook. Oh, well. I'm glad I am still on Twitter.

Yong Zhao
University of Oregon

Yong Zhao is presidential chair and professor at the College of Education, University of Oregon. He is author of *World Class Learners: Educating Creative and Entrepreneurial Students.* You can follow him on Twitter at @yongzhao.uo or on his website: http://zhaolearning.com.

Preface

dvances in technology have led to changes in the way people communicate, collaborate, solve problems, create projects, and consume content. These changes have shifted how key stakeholders in education (parents, students, community members) prefer to receive information and communicate with schools.

The increasing dominance technology plays in our lives can easily be experienced through behavioral observations of professionals, businesses, parents, children, and even grandparents. The number of adult Internet users with profiles on social network sites has more than quadrupled over a four-year span—from 8% in 2005 to 35% now—according to the Pew Internet and American Life Project's December 2008 tracking survey (Pew Internet and American Life Project, 2009). Have school structures and procedures taken these shifts into account? More important, do leaders know how to adapt to these shifts and thus lead meaningful, sustainable change in their schools?

AUDIENCE

The primary audience for the book are school leaders (supervisors, assistant principals, principals, directors of curriculum, and superintendents). Professors of higher education can also integrate this book in their preparation programs, as many people would agree that exposure to this style of leadership is desperately needed. Even though the book will be directed at school leaders because they have the decision-making power to implement schoolwide and districtwide changes, teachers can easily incorporate the principles at the classroom level to improve their communication with their students, colleagues, parents, and community members.

THE CALL

Leaders today must establish a vision and implement a strategic process that creates a teaching and learning culture that provides students with essential skill sets—creativity, communication, collaboration, critical thinking, problem solving, technological proficiency, and global awareness—commonly referred to as twenty-first-century skills, although it has become obsolete as we are now well into the twenty-first century. These skills and processes should be at the heart of every decision a leader makes and are key to providing students with the tools to succeed in jobs that have not yet been created. Consistent innovation, effective integration of technology, meaningful professional development, connecting beyond the walls of a brick-and-mortar building, and an open mind are all mandatory duties of a leader in the digital age.

The call to prepare students for the unknown jobs of tomorrow is made more difficult as mounting challenges such as budget cuts, Common Core Standards, value-added evaluation of staff using standardized test scores, and what seems like a relentless attack on the profession of education have taken their toll on staff morale. Quality leadership therefore becomes imperative in order to cultivate a school culture whose primary focus is on the learning and achievement of each and every student while anticipating needed changes in a society that is evolving at a dizzying pace.

It can also be argued that these changes have created a new type of learner that schools are entrusted with educating, as well as key stakeholders with shifting needs in terms of how they prefer to communicate with schools. In this digital age, we are experiencing amazing advances in educational technology that have the potential to enhance the teaching and learning process, as well as establish powerful connections with our communities and among an array of stakeholders. These advances have also unlocked the creative potential of many students, teachers, and administrators.

The challenge for school leaders is to acknowledge these societal changes and embrace them. If schools continue to follow an outdated educational model focusing on preparation for an industrialized workforce, they run the risk of becoming irrelevant to our students and communities. As Kelly, McCain, and Jukes (2009) point out, there is a fundamental disconnect between students and the schools they attend. Why are schools not meeting the diverse learning needs of digital learners? Do school leaders leverage available technology and social media to do what they do better? Are our decisions and behaviors taking into account future shifts and changes? Why are so many slow or fearful to change? If these pressing questions are not squarely addressed by leaders, our system of education will continue to devolve into irrelevancy and inadequacy.

Digital leadership consists of a dynamic combination of mindset, behaviors, and skills that are employed to change and enhance school culture through the use of technology. In the early 2000s, the term *Web 2.0* was coined. Wikipedia defines Web 2.0 as

> a perceived second generation of web development and design, that facilitates communication, secure information sharing, interoperability, and collaboration on the World Wide Web. Web 2.0 concepts have led to the development and evolution of web-based communities, hosted services, and applications such as social-networking sites, video-sharing sites, wikis, blogs, and folksonomies. ("Web 2.0," 2013)

According to Bryan Alexander, the Director of Research for the National Institute for Technology and Liberal Education and a frequent commentator on technology trends in education, Web 2.0, a term which was popularized by Tim O'Reilly in late 2004, refers to those Web technologies that allow users to easily produce "digital content that can be copied, moved, altered, remixed, and linked, based on the needs, interests, and abilities of users" (Alexander, 2008, p. 151). Digital leaders embrace Web 2.0 technology as a means to enhance leadership and professional practice.

As leaders began to evolve and take advantage of Web 2.0 tools, they began to embrace change, demonstrate transparency, increase engagement, employ collaboration, focus heavily on sharing, initiate global dialogue, and build community. Leaders quickly found the value in a plethora of Web 2.0 tools, commonly known as social media, to enhance traditional aspects of leadership (i.e., management, instruction, and communication) while forging new pathways to initiate change leading to transformation. Many would argue that this leadership style is still prevalent today.

The Web, like leadership, continues to evolve, however, and the way it is accessed evolves as well. This has led to Web 3.0, a term originated by John Markoff of *The New York Times* and defined as

> a supposed third generation of Internet-based services that collectively comprise what might be called "the intelligent Web"—such as those using semantic webs, microformats, natural language search, data-mining, machine learning, recommendation agents, and artificial intelligence technologies—which emphasize[s] machine-facilitated understanding of information in order to provide a more productive and intuitive user experience. (as cited in Spivack, n.d.)

Digital leadership takes into account recent changes such as ubiquitous connectivity, open-source technology, mobile devices, and personalization. It represents a dramatic shift from how schools have been run and structured for over a century, as what started out as a personal use of technology has become systemic to every facet of leadership. Bret Simmons (2010) sums up the evolution of the Web nicely:

- Web 1.0 is informational,
- Web 2.0 is relational,
- Web 3.0 is anticipatory.

Digital leadership can thus be defined as establishing direction, influencing others, initiating sustainable change though the access to information, and establishing relationships in order to anticipate changes pivotal to school success in the future. Leaders must learn to better anticipate the learning needs of students and staff, their desire for information from stakeholders, and the necessary elements of school culture that address both the Common Core Standards and essential skill sets. They must also be "change savvy" (Herold & Fedor, 2008), which involves

- careful entry into the new setting;
- listening to and learning from those who have been there or been at it longer;
- engaging in fact finding and joint problem solving;
- carefully, rather than rashly, diagnosing the situation;
- forthrightly addressing people's concerns;
- being enthusiastic, genuine, and sincere about the change circumstances;
- obtaining support for what needs to be fixed or improved; and
- developing a credible plan for making a fix or improvement.

CENTRAL PURPOSE AND FOCUS OF THIS BOOK

Digital Leadership: Changing Paradigms for Changing Times presents a framework for leaders to harness the power of digital technologies in order to create school cultures that are transparent, relevant, meaningful, engaging, and inspiring. In order to set the stage for increasing achievement and to establish a greater sense of community pride for the work being done in our schools, we must begin to change the way we lead. To do this, leaders must understand the origins of fear and misconceptions that often surround the use of technology such as social media and mobile devices. Once the fears and misconceptions are placed on the table, leaders can begin to establish a vision for the effective use of technology to improve numerous facets of leadership. The challenge for school leaders is why, how, and where to begin. Digital leadership is not about flashy tools, but a strategic mindset that leverages available resources to improve what we do while anticipating the changes needed to cultivate a school culture focused on engagement and achievement. This book will present a new construct of leadership that grows out of the leader's symbiotic relationship with technology.

This book provides leaders with the concrete evidence used to transform the teaching and learning culture in New Milford High School in a relatively short period of time. It tells the story of how I radically changed my beliefs on how a school should be structured and function, with the end result being sustainable change in programs, instruction, behaviors, and leadership involving technology. It examines how shifting a leadership style from one of mandates, directives, and buy-in to one grounded in empowerment, support, and embracement is the key to sustainable change.

The Pillars of Digital Leadership

Digital Leadership: Changing Paradigms for Changing Times outlines what I refer to as the "Pillars of Digital Leadership." These are the specific areas embedded in the culture of all schools that can be improved or enhanced through the use of available technology, especially social media. They are

- **Communication**: Leaders can now provide stakeholders with relevant information in real time through a variety of devices. No longer do static, one-way methods such as newsletters and websites suffice. Discussion will focus on types of information that can be communicated through various free social media tools and simple implementation strategies.
- **Public relations**: If we don't tell our story, someone else will, and more often than not, another's version will not be the one we want told. Leaders need to become story-tellers-in-chief. This section will focus on how leaders can form the foundation of a positive public relations platform using free social media tools. By doing so, they create the means by which they share all of the positives associated with their schools and create a much-needed level of transparency in an age of negative rhetoric toward education.
- **Branding**: Businesses have long understood the value of brand and its impact on current and potential consumers. Leaders can leverage social media tools to create a positive brand presence that emphasizes the positive aspects of school culture, increases community pride, and helps to attract/retain families when looking for a place to send their children to school.
- **Student engagement/learning**: We cannot expect to see increases in achievement if students are not learning. Students who are not engaged are not likely to be learning. Leaders need to understand that schools should reflect real life and allow students to apply what they have learned through the use of the tools they are using outside of school. Pulling from real-world examples at New Milford High School and other innovative schools across the world, a blueprint is provided for effective technology integration ideas and strategies that are cost-effective and focus on enhancing essential skill sets—communication, collaboration, creativity, media

literacy, global connectedness, critical thinking, and problem solving.

- **Professional growth/development**: With the rise of social media, schools no longer have to be silos of information and leaders do not have to feel like they are on isolated islands that lack support and feedback. This section discusses how leaders can form their own Personal Learning Network (PLN) to meet their diverse learning needs; acquire resources; access knowledge; receive feedback; connect with experts in the field of education as well as practitioners; and discuss proven strategies to improve teaching, learning, and leadership. Readers will learn how to develop their own PLN for free and access this newly acquired, priceless resource anywhere at any time. Digital leadership ensures that leaders are accessing the latest trends, research, and ideas in the field.

- **Reenvisioning learning spaces and environments**: Once leaders understand the pillars and how to use them to initiate sustainable change, the next step is to begin to transform learning spaces and environments that support essential skill sets and are aligned with the real world. Leaders must begin to establish a vision and strategic plan to create an entire school building dedicated to learning in an ever so more digital world. In order to do so, leaders must be knowledgeable of the characteristics and dynamics that embody innovative learning spaces and environments.

- **Opportunity**: It is important for leaders to consistently seek out ways to improve existing programs, resources, and professional development. This section highlights how to leverage connections made through technology and increase opportunities to make improvements across multiple areas of school culture. Leaders will see how the other six pillars connect and work together to bring about unprecedented opportunities impossible otherwise, such as acquiring donations or resources worth thousands of dollars, authentic learning experiences for students, and the formation of innovative conferences.

Leaders need to be the catalysts for change in each of these pillars. Each is critical in its own right to transforming and sustaining a positive school culture. This book breaks down each pillar, uses research to emphasize its importance and value, and provides an overview of specific tools and strategies that can be used regardless of budget obstacles. I use not only my experiences and successes in each of these areas, but also those of other innovative leaders from across the country whom I have met through social media. These practitioner vignettes offer powerful voices that establish a context for each pillar and illustrate the *why* and *how* so that readers will be able to implement the strategies in their own contexts. The Appendix contains useful reproducibles that leaders can begin to use immediately to enhance their professional practice. By addressing each of these pillars, leaders can begin changing and transforming their respective schools into ones that prepare learners with essential digital-age skills while engaging a variety of stakeholders.

After reading this book, you will be able to

- Identify obstacles to change and specific solutions to overcome them in order to transform schools in the digital age
- Use digital tools and leadership practices to enhance school culture and improve stakeholder relations
- Leverage the real-time Web to grow professionally like never before
- Utilize practical strategies from practicing school leaders that will provide a context for digital leadership in action

Acknowledgments

Like many pieces of writing, *Digital Leadership: Changing Paradigms for Changing Times* has been a labor of love for Eric. For him, social media were a catalyst for conversation that not only provided him with ideas and inspiration, but also connected him with some of the most amazing educational leaders in the world: leaders such as David Britten, Dwight Carter, John Carver, Spike Cook, George Couros, Peter DeWitt, Robert Dillon, Lyn Hill, Patrick Larkin, Joe Mazza, and Pam Moran. Each of them models the essence of digital leadership and continuously provide Eric with the support and guidance to lead change and grow professionally. One could not forget business maven Trish Rubin, who taught Eric about the importance of branding in education. Her insight and continuous mentoring have given Eric a fresh look at what education can and should be.

As much as digital influences and influencers played a role in the development of this book, the traditional elements have been just as important. Almost every idea and strategy laid out in the book originated and/or evolved at New Milford High School (NMHS). Eric will forever be indebted to the NMHS community—students, teachers, administrators, parents, and other stakeholders—for their support, confidence, feedback, and inspiration. His family has also been instrumental with their patience and advice on how to craft a manuscript that not only makes sense, but also has value to an array of educators.

Finally, Eric would like to thank the staff of Corwin: Executive Editor Arnis Burvikovs, who would not take no for an answer and convinced Eric to write this book focusing on his work as a digital leader; Senior Associate Editor Desiree Bartlett, who provided invaluable feedback and suggestions on how to improve the manuscript; Sarah Payne-Mills, whose keen eye and sound suggestions greatly assisted in creating this valuable resource; and Editorial Assistant Ariel Price, who kept Eric in the know with due dates, permissions, and other materials needed for the book.

PUBLISHER'S ACKNOWLEDGMENTS

Corwin gratefully acknowledges the contributions of the following reviewers:

Natalie Bernasconi, La Paz Middle School NBCT Teacher
Technology Literacy Coach
University of California, Santa Cruz Lecturer
Google Certified Teacher
Salinas, CA

David G. Daniels, Principal
Susquehanna Valley Senior High School
Conklin, NY

Harry Dickens, Director of Technology
Arkansas Public School Resource Center
Little Rock, AR

Addie Gaines, Principal
Kirbyville Elementary School
Kirbyville, MO

Jessica Johnson, Principal and District Assessment Coordinator
Dodgeland Elementary School
Juneau, WI

Scott McLeod, Associate Professor and Founding Director, CASTLE
University of Kentucky
Lexington, KY

Tanna Nicely, Assistant Principal
Sarah Moore Greene Elementary School
Knoxville, TN

Matt Renwick, Principal
Howe Elementary School
Wisconsin Rapids, WI

John Robinson, The 21st Century Principal
Discovery High School
Newton, NC

Bess Scott, Director of Elementary Education
Lincoln Public Schools
Lincoln, NE

About the Author

Eric Sheninger is the principal of New Milford High School, located in Bergen County, New Jersey. He is passionate about establishing and fostering learning environments that are student centered, collaborative, flexible, and capable of preparing all learners to succeed in the twenty-first century.

As an educational administrator, he firmly believes that effective communication, listening, support, shared decision making, and the integration of technology are essential elements for the transformation of school cultures. Eric has emerged as an innovative leader in the use of social media and Web 2.0 technology as tools to engage students, improve communication with stakeholders, and help educators grow professionally. Eric is a 2012 National Association of Secondary School Principals Digital Principal Award recipient; 2012 PDK Emerging Leader Award winner; recipient of Learning Forward's Excellence in Professional Practice Award (2012); Google Certified Teacher; Adobe Education Leader; ASCD 2011 Conference Scholar; blogger for the *Huffington Post*; coauthor of *Communicating and Connecting With Social Media* and *What Principals Need to Know About Teaching and Learning Science;* and was named to the National School Boards Association "20 to Watch" list in 2010 for technology leadership. He now presents and speaks nationally to assist other school leaders in embracing and effectively utilizing technology. His blog, A Principal's Reflections, earned Best School Administrator Blog in 2011 from Edublogs.

Eric began his career in education as a science teacher at Watchung Hills Regional High School in Warren, New Jersey. He then transitioned into the field of educational administration, first as an athletic director and supervisor of physical education and health and then as vice principal in the New Milford School District. During his administrative career, he has served as district affirmative action officer and is the current president of the New Milford Administrators' Association.

Eric earned a bachelor of science degree from Salisbury University, a bachelor of science from the University of Maryland Eastern Shore, and a master of education in educational administration from East Stroudsburg University. To learn more about Eric's work, visit ericsheninger.com, or follow @NMHS_Principal on Twitter.

A Day in the Life of a Digital Leader

I am a digital leader. My day starts off like any other. I arrive at school, greet the administrative assistants, and then boot up my computer. For the next couple of minutes, I put the finishing touches on the staff e-mail message of the day. This is the point at which things might be a bit different for me when compared to other administrators.

As I work on the daily e-mail, my Twitter stream is also visible though an application called TweetDeck. I browse the many tweets from members of my PLN to look for resources to include in the e-mail to my staff. On this particular day, I found an exciting list of Web-based tools that my staff could integrate into their lessons. I then quickly finish up my e-mail, send it off, and again browse my Twitter and Google+ streams to catch up on the latest developments in education.

My next morning tasks consist of updating announcements for students on a Google Doc that they can access on the school website. Once these are finished, I post the link on our school's Twitter and Facebook pages, and a notification is sent out through our official school app the NMHS students helped to develop. Prior to homeroom beginning, I update all of the school social media accounts to keep all stakeholders abreast of the latest developments and news related to the school.

The day finally begins around 8:00 AM. Armed with my smartphone and tablet, I begin walking the halls, observing classes, and conducting walk-throughs. Throughout all of these activities, I look for opportunities to share student work and accomplishments using social media tools such as Twitter, Instagram, YouTube, and Facebook. I also love to capture innovative lessons and projects that my teachers have implemented where technology has been effectively integrated. On this particular day, a teacher was using Poll Everywhere to have students text in their answers to a do-now question. There is nothing more exciting than seeing students using their mobile learning devices to answer questions. This not only enhances the learning experience but also prepares my students for the real world, where devices are essential tools in many professions.

I eventually pop back into my office to attend to the usual management tasks that often consume school leaders. However, time is quickly allocated to peruse through and comment on articles that my digital journalism students just posted on The Lance (thelance.net). I usually learn about this as they post updates on the Twitter page that was created for the class in order to report stories in real time and promote their work.

During lunch, my administrative team and I take turns supervising in order to free up teachers so that they can use the time to learn and grow professionally. As we are a Bring Your Own Device (BYOD) school, students are freely using their devices to socialize, complete homework, conduct research, or organize their day. I seize the opportunity to get Minecraft tips for my son, but also to catch up on completing observation write-ups using either my laptop or tablet. Thanks to our school's Wi-Fi, I can work seamlessly anywhere in the building. Working in the presence of my students is an added bonus.

The afternoon is usually comprised of the same tasks and instructional duties as the morning. As I travel the halls, I peek into classrooms and see students using their mobile learning devices to take pictures of notes the teacher has placed on the board, create learning artifacts, and collaborate on assignments. As the student day ends, I work to make sure every managerial task has been completed. I then use the next couple of hours to blog about the great things I saw during the day and catch up on the chatter in social media spaces to acquire resources for my teachers and improve professional practice.

I am a digital leader, connected not only to my school, but to a global network of educators that has evolved into my most treasured resource. This network consists of tens of thousands of educators from five different continents. As a building leader in a small school, I still attend to and complete major job tasks such as observations, walk-throughs, Common Core alignment, preparing for new teacher evaluations, budgeting, master scheduling, meetings, and other managerial issues. What distinguishes me from most other school principals, though, is that I have learned to integrate a variety of digital tools and strategies to enhance all the facets of how I lead. Digital leadership is not an add-on, but a complement to everything that I do as a principal. It is not a time sap, either; instead, it is a different way of leading that is richer, more effective, more efficient, and better informed.

1

The Evolving Educational Landscape

"Today's kids are born digital—born into a media-rich, networked world of infinite possibilities. But their digital lifestyle is about more than just cool gadgets; it's about engagement, self-directed learning, creativity, and empowerment."

—Edutopia (2012)

INCREASED ONLINE ACCESS, MOBILE DEVICES, AND CONNECTIVITY

Societal shifts involving technology are beginning to have a profound impact on teaching, infrastructure, resources, stakeholder relations, and our learners. The opportunities include greater access to rich, multimedia content; the increasing use of online courses that offer classes not otherwise available; the widespread availability of mobile computing devices that can access the Internet; the expanding role of social networking

1

tools for learning and professional development; and the growing interest in the power of digital games for more personalized learning (*Education Week*, 2011). Online access in particular has become embedded in the routines of daily life across the industrialized world (Livingstone, 2008). Understanding these shifts is key to developing a teaching and learning culture that best meets the needs of our students, while improving how we connect with our other stakeholders.

There are some interesting statistics that highlight people's use of technology. The average amount of time Americans spend online increased dramatically over the first decade of the twenty-first century, from 2.7 hours per *week* in 2000 to almost 2.6 hours per *day* in 2010. And that's the average; high school students are much more active users of Web 2.0 technologies (Rodriguez, 2010, p. 56). More than half (55%) of all online American youths, age twelve to seventeen, use online social networking sites, according to a national survey of teenagers conducted by the Pew Internet and American Life Project (2007). Three years later, this same project found that nearly three-quarters (73%) of online teens and an equal number (72%) of young adults use social network sites. Some 40% of adults 30 and older used the social networking sites (Pew Internet and American Life Project, 2010).

Other behaviors and trends are emerging as the world becomes more digital. In 2011, 71% of children, age eleven to sixteen, had their own games console at home, spending an average of 1.7 hours per day using this technology (Childwise, 2012). A study conducted by Andreu Casero-Ripollés (2012) found that young people's news consumption is oriented toward new media, especially social networks, while newspaper readership among young people is in decline. As a consequence, newspapers are no longer the primary source of information in the digital context (Lipani, 2008). Wi-Fi has become a mainstream wireless technology that provides Internet access at home to a wide variety of consumer electronics and mobile devices. Coupled with the proliferation of Wi-Fi–enabled devices, the continued expansion of broadband services provides a solid foundation for further growth in home Wi-Fi adoption. Approximately 25% of all Internet-connected households in the world now have wireless home networks, which is about 439 million households worldwide (Strategy Analytics, 2012). The average U.S. household owns five devices connected to the Internet via Wi-Fi, wired, or cellular networks (Bloomberg, 2012).

These statistics verify a growing trend that the majority of our students, stakeholders, and teachers are engaged in online spaces and have ample means to access the Internet. Within these spaces they are creating, communicating, collaborating, and discussing. This is occurring on mainstream social media sites such as Facebook, YouTube, Twitter, LinkedIn, and Skype, as well as some relatively new ones such as Instagram, Pinterest, Tumblr, and Google+. Individuals find value in the amount of time spent using social media to connect with friends, read digital content, play video games, and create their own unique content. It is hard to deny the high level of engagement and interactivity that is taking place, all of which supports many of the essential skill sets that schools claim they want to enhance. This is the world into which our students are being born and within which all members of society are immersed. The conversation needs to shift from one that focuses on digital natives and immigrants to one that looks at the fact that technology now permeates virtually every facet of society. As the Internet continues to evolve, users will continue to adapt.

All these statistics paint a general picture of society's use, reliance, and infatuation with the Internet. Access to information in real time has become the standard, spearheaded by the continuous rise and evolution of social media sites. With the proliferation of mobile technology (smartphones, tablets, e-readers) and advances in wireless connectivity, it can be assumed that many of the statistics cited above are actually much greater. The following are some global statistics on mobile devices compiled by mobiThinking (2012):

- At the end of 2011, there were 6 billion mobile subscriptions. That is equivalent to 87% of the world population and is a huge increase from 5.4 billion mobile subscriptions in 2010 and 4.7 billion in 2009.
- There were 11.1% more mobile devices sold in 2011 than in 2010.
- Total smartphone sales in 2011 reached 472 million units, up 58% from 2010. This makes smartphones 31% of all handsets shipped.
- The IDC predicts that 122.3 million tablets will be sold in 2012, rising to 172.4 million units in 2013 and 282.7 million units in 2016. By 2016, Windows will have made significant gains: iOS share will be 49.7%, Android 39.7%, and Windows 10.3%.

Society has a craving for accessing the Internet for a variety of purposes and now possesses the means to connect in many ways. In response to these shifts, some educational leaders have begun to recognize that the current structure and function of institutions of learning are not in tune with the real world that is continuously advancing beyond the walls of schools. Finally, conversations are taking place on how schools and leaders can take advantage of the phenomena associated with this digital-age renaissance. Once sparsely connected, we have now seen school investments in wireless networks that connect throughout buildings to the Internet. Having the infrastructure in place is one thing; using it to advance learning and enhance other facets of leadership is another. CoSN and the Metri Group recently conducted a survey of school administrators for the MacArthur Foundation and found that districts across the country are wary of venturing into the world of social networking during school hours (Lemke et al., 2009). The results of this survey are troubling, as we now have a generation of learners who are comfortable with and enthusiastic about using Web 2.0 technologies to collaborate and participate in the World Wide Web as creators rather than consumers (Rosen & Nelson, 2008).

As a result of the lack of initiative, fear, unwillingness to change, or not knowing where to begin on the part of school leaders, a natural disconnect has formed between key stakeholders and schools, because people are now heavily invested in using digital technologies for both personal and professional reasons. The longer this disconnect continues, the more meaningless and irrelevant our schools become to our students. It is time to transform schools into vibrant learning communities that are connected and allow access to numerous social media tools that can unleash the creativity of our learners. This will increase engagement and, ultimately, achievement. By understanding how reliant all stakeholders are on the Internet, leaders can develop strategies to better communicate information, enhance public relations, collaborate with other practitioners, discover opportunities to improve school culture, and be open to a nonstop pathway of new, innovative ideas.

ADVANCEMENTS IN EDUCATIONAL TECHNOLOGY AND CURRENT TRENDS

The Internet is not the only thing that continues to change. The advancement of existing technologies as well as the introduction of new tools has created a rich market for schools to utilize. Schools adopt educational technology to increase student engagement in learning; improve learning (i.e., higher standardized test scores); improve the economic viability of students (i.e., increasing students' abilities to succeed in a twenty-first-century work environment through teaming, technology fluency, and high productivity); close the digital divide by increasing technology literacy in all students; increase relevance and real-world application of academics; and build twenty-first-century skills such as critical thinking and sound reasoning, global awareness, communication skills, information and visual literacy, scientific reasoning, productivity, and creativity (Lemke, Coughlin, & Reifsneider, 2009).

There seems to be no shortage of technology tools that are being used to increase student engagement, access and manage information, foster creativity, assess, curate content, and aid in conceptual mastery. Whether it is from societal pressures, marketing techniques, or a shift in vision, educational technology has become more prevalent in schools. Some schools have been adept at keeping up with those changes, while many others are falling far behind, creating a digital divide based largely on the quality of educational technology, rather than just simple access to the Internet (*Education Week*, 2011). How it is ultimately used and its relative effectiveness in improving teaching, learning, and leadership will be discussed later in this book.

Desktops and laptops have long been considered the standard when it comes to educational technology in schools. As these devices have evolved, their prices have dropped, making them much more attainable within school budgets. Many computer suppliers have instituted lease programs, which make their products even more attractive in these difficult economic times. In addition to computers, there are many common educational technologies that are being utilized in schools today and have begun to reshape pedagogy, conceptual mastery, professional development, and content consumption.

Interactive Whiteboards (IWBs)

Considered by many to be a standard in schools nowadays, the IWB is a presentation device connected to a computer and projector. It is typically mounted to a wall, but can also be configured to a rolling stand. A projector displays the computer's image in the IWB, and users can control the image using finger or interactive marker devices designed by the manufacturer. The appeal of IWBs lies in the opportunity for use of dynamic, interactive images, animations, video, and text of a size visible to an entire classroom (Lemke, Coughlin, & Reifsneider, 2009). The research has also found that IWBs can have a positive impact on learning. Haystead and Marzano (2009) conducted eighty-five studies in fifty different schools and found large percentile gains in student achievement under the following conditions: The teacher had ten or more years of teaching experience, had used the IWB for two years or more, used the IWB 75% to 80% of the time in the classroom, and had possessed high confidence in using the technology.

Tablets

Tablets have exploded into the marketplace and have begun to be integrated into schools. These devices are more portable than laptops, and they are smaller and cheaper, which makes them very attractive centerpieces for 1:1 initiatives— that is, where every student has a device. Recent advances in digital publishing have resulted in many traditional textbooks now being available on tablet devices for a fraction of the cost. Apple has dominated the tablet market with its iPad, which launched in 2012. As of 2013, the Apple App Store supports over 700,000 apps for the iPad. Even with the iPad's dominance, the tablet market has become saturated with stiff competition from Android tablets such as those manufactured by Samsung. Tablets are a powerful educational tool because they provide access to informational tools for learning, and productivity can be used for research. In addition, they have the ability to replace traditional textbooks. For example, students and educators can access iTunes U for free and access entire courses of educational content for K–12 schools.

Document Cameras

These devices work very similarly to their ancestor, the overhead projector. Document cameras are connected to a projector in order to display the image of anything put underneath the camera, which is the main function of an overhead projector. What makes these devices more dynamic is their ability to record both video and sound, a useful feature that allows teachers to capture lessons and notes to make available to their students through a website. They are cost-effective, small, and portable. Some models even use wireless technology, so they don't have to be hardwired to a projector.

Chromebooks

Google developed this one-of-a-kind device that contains no operating system or hard drive. When the computer boots up, it connects directly to the Internet, and the entire process takes around ten seconds. They are very cost-effective, being hundreds of dollars less than laptops, popular tablets, and even netbooks. Users can create a free Google profile and log on to any Chromebook to access their Google Docs, favorite websites, or Web-based applications that they have added to their account. The major drawback to the Chromebook is that if the Internet is down, the device has limited functionality.

Apple TV

The allure of Apple TV is its ability to mirror images from any Apple device to a projector or television. The Apple TV device is connected directly to either an HDMI projector or HDMI port on a television. Once the mirroring setting is enabled on the Apple device, the image appears on the television or projector screen. Many schools have now begun purchasing and using an Apple TV, HDMI projector, and iPad to create a wireless IWB. Best of all, this setup costs about $1,500 less than a mounted IWB, but maintains all of the benefits of this technology.

3-D Content

There has been a consistent rise in the use of 3-D content to enhance teaching and learning. From specialized projectors to visual learning solutions, content providers are continuing to build upon their products to immerse students in virtual learning environments where they not only see, but hear and feel as well. These technologies are having a positive impact on learning. JTM Concepts of Rock Island, Illinois, began collecting data on the educational impact of its 3-D content in 2003. The results were impressive. Data showed that students who observed the 3-D simulations made a big jump from their prelesson to postlesson test scores while outperforming control groups who received traditional instruction (Gordon, 2010). A smaller study showed that students who observed the 3-D lesson improved an average of 32% from pretest to posttest, with substantial gains in every subgroup.

Cloud Computing

This term refers to any hosted service that can be accessed over the Internet. Many schools are now investing in virtual servers, which are much more cost-effective than traditional ones. For schools and administrators, the "cloud" has become a more effective and efficient way of managing documents, projects, and general information, as they can all be stored virtually and accessed anywhere. This has resulted in the adoption of Google's suite of free tools by many schools and educators alike. As cost-effective and enticing as cloud computing is, many schools fear losing control of private student information. The Family Educational Rights and Privacy Act (FERPA) (20 U.S.C. § 1232g; 34 CFR Part 99) is a federal law that protects the privacy of student education records. The law applies to all schools that receive funds under an applicable program of the U.S. Department of Education. FERPA does not offer much guidance for schools on the selection and maintenance of cloud providers and the resulting relationships. The good news for school leaders, though, is that nothing in FERPA prevents schools from using cloud-based services, and schools across the country have embraced these solutions. When contracting any cloud computing solution, it must be clear that the party to whom the information is disclosed will not disclose the information to any other party without the prior consent of the parent or eligible student. If this condition is not met, it is a violation of FERPA.

Web 2.0 Applications

Within the cloud are many applications commonly referred to as Web 2.0 tools. Many of these tools are free and work to promote essential skill sets such as collaboration, communication, creativity, and global awareness. Popular applications include Voicethread, Wordle, Animoto, Glogster, Prezi, Padlet, Poll Everywhere, Celly, and blogging platforms. Social media tools such as Twitter, Google+, wikis, blogs, and digital discussion forums are now becoming widely accepted as means to grow professionally. The only downside of Web 2.0 applications is that they are generally grouped together with mainstream social media sites such as Facebook and YouTube. As a result, many schools block them and prohibit access, feeling that their use is a violation of the Child Internet Protection Act (CIPA). Congress enacted CIPA in 2000 to address concerns over children accessing inappropriate content over the Internet. The Federal Communications Commission (FCC, 2011) provides details that schools need to know about CIPA:

> Schools must certify that they have an Internet safety policy that includes technology protection measures. The protection measures must block or filter Internet access to pictures that are: (a) obscene; (b) child pornography; or (c) harmful to minors (for computers that are accessed by minors). Before adopting this Internet safety policy, schools and libraries must provide reasonable notice and hold at least one public hearing or meeting to address the proposal.

So why are the majority of schools blocking these amazing tools? School leaders are well aware of CIPA but are misinformed when it comes to the access of Web 2.0 applications. All that CIPA requires in order for schools to be eligible to receive e-Rate funding is that inappropriate websites are blocked.

In a 2011 interview, the Department of Education's Director of Education Technology, Karen Cator, explained that accessing YouTube and similar social media sites is not a violation of CIPA, and Web 2.0 sites do not have to be blocked for teachers (Barseghian, 2011). The takeaway here is that leaders must become advocates for the use of Web 2.0 applications in schools, working with all stakeholders to create an environment focusing on responsible use. They need to be active in creating and sustaining a safe online environment for students and Acceptable Use Policies (AUPs) that address misuse, and also ensuring that adequate supervision is provided at all times.

Mobile Technology

As mentioned earlier in this chapter, mobile technology (i.e., mobile phones, tablets, e-readers) have exploded into the marketplace and into homes. This trend has not gone unnoticed in the education world. Schools and leaders are beginning to see the value in purchasing mobile technology for 1:1 initiatives, while others are opting for more cost-effective programs that utilize the technology that students already own. These latter initiatives are commonly referred to as either Bring Your Own Device (BYOD) or Bring Your Own Technology (BYOT) programs. Regardless of the acronym, digital-rich environments are created as leaders begin to rethink existing policies that prohibited access to sites that have educational value and prevented use of student-owned devices that can be leveraged for learning. Mobile learning devices hold great potential since they can be used by a variety of stakeholder groups for assessment, content curation, research, organization, collaboration on projects, classroom walk-throughs, and observations.

Video Conferencing

As the Internet has evolved, so has video-conferencing technology. Long past are the days when this tool was only available to schools in affluent areas or through sparse grants. All one now needs is a webcam-enabled device (i.e., desktop, laptop, tablet, or smartphone), Internet connection, and either a program or app (e.g., Skype, iChat, Adobe Connect, Google Hangouts) to create a video feed. Schools now have the means to conduct virtual field trips, connect with authors, and collaborate with colleagues from across the globe. Using tools like Ustream (www.ustream.tv), schools can not only broadcast live events, but can even archive the footage for viewing at a later time.

OpenCourseWare (OCW) and Massive Open Online Courses (MOOCs)

One of the major recent advancements in educational technology has been the availability of entire courses from some of the nation's most prestigious universities and professors free of charge. The movement began with the Massachusetts Institute of Technology (MIT), which believed that making OCW available would enhance human learning worldwide by the availability of a web of knowledge (Vest, 2004). Harvard, Yale, Stanford, and the University of Michigan are just a sample of some of the universities offering access to their courses online through MOOCs. OCW is comprised of content in the form of university lectures, notes, and assignments with little emphasis on cohesiveness. MOOCs, on the other hand, are structured around lengthy courses aligned to online learning. In this setting, lectures are scheduled by professors or facilitators with associated deadlines, assignments, assessments, and community engagement. The accessibility and quality of OCW holds the promise of providing students and educators with more personalized learning options that can cater to diverse needs. In addition to universities across the globe, other organizations such as NIXTY (nixty.com) and Connexions (cnx.org) provide access to even more OCW options.

Virtual Schooling

Also known as cyberschooling or distance learning, this is a service that schools can invest in, available to students anywhere at any time. Traditional schools can increase their current course catalogues by hundreds of new courses that cater to student interest. Key characteristics of virtual schools include credit attainment to complement studies at a local campus, and ability of students to work at their own pace; instruction is available year round, courses are taught by highly qualified teachers, and there is a wide range of courses available that are updated frequently (Kelly, McCain, & Jukes, 2009).

Electronic delivery provided by a virtual school can occur using synchronous communication, in which class members participate at the same time, or asynchronous communication, where participants are separated by time (Mielke, 1999). In a synchronous course, students meet with a live instructor at set times. The content is delivered using videoconference technology, and students submit their assignments to the instructor when due. In an asynchronous course, students can access the learning materials at times convenient for them, but all work and assignments are due within a specified period of time. As in a synchronous course, assignments are sent to a certified teacher. Virtual schooling offers students considerable benefits, including convenience of time and place (LeLoup & Ponterio, 2000). Popular providers include the VHS Collaborative (thevhscollaborative.org) and the Florida Virtual School (www.flvs.net/Pages/default.aspx).

Gaming

Long thought only to be a distraction, current research is beginning to tell a different story about gaming in education. James Gee (2007) derived a set of thirty-six learning principles from his study of the complex, self-directed learning each player undertakes as he or she encounters and masters a new game. He suggests that adherence to these principles could transform learning in schools both for teachers and faculty and, most important, for students. Steve Johnson (2006) even found that video games, from *Tetris* to *The Sims* to *Grand Theft Auto*, have been shown to raise IQ scores and develop cognitive abilities, skills that even books can't foster. Some innovative schools have begun to seize the opportunity with educational gaming by investing in popular game consoles such as Nintendo Wii and Microsoft's Xbox 360 Kinect. Both of these systems can be used to support tactile and kinesthetic learning styles. This is significant, as ongoing research shows that students learn more quickly and easily with instruction across multiple modalities or through a variety of media (Lemke, 2008). One of the hottest gaming trends is *Minecraft* (minecraft.net), a world-building game that some educators have embraced to teach physics, geography, and the English language. Another exciting tool is VR Quest, where students can design 3-D virtual reality games aligned to the Common Core Standards. To learn more, visit www.vrquest.net.

A New Learner

> *"Our students have changed radically. Today's students are no longer the people our educational system was designed to teach."*
>
> —Mark Prensky (2001, p. 1)

The world has changed, as have the learners that schools are responsible for educating. They may be referred to as the iGeneration, Millennials, or Generation Y. Whether we like it or not, students today are immersed in an environment rich in digital media and tools. These tools have become status symbols, means of communication, and digital-age organizers. Many people would agree they have also become a student's nerve center, because so much of their lives are now influenced by the tools of the age. The attraction ultimately begins at a young and innocent age. All one has to do is observe a toddler with an iPad or a slightly older child building a virtual world in *The SIMS*. Observe enough, and it is tough to deny how technology does not spark curiosity, ignite ingenuity, and foster collaboration.

Students are engaged in their digital worlds, and they are learning without us. It has become a much more active process due to that ease of accessing information on the Internet and a wide range of tools that support constructivist learning. Students are constructing meaning through the use of technology in ways that are relevant, meaningful, and fun.

Leaders of schools need to acknowledge that learners today are "wired" differently as a result of the experiential learning that is taking place outside of school. The learning styles of the active, digital learner conflict with traditional teaching styles and preferences. How can we possibly meet the needs of these unique learners if our practices are suited for a time that has long since passed? Ian Jukes, Ted McCain, and Lee Crockett (2010) provide the following characteristics of learners today and the resulting disconnects that they are experiencing in schools:

- Digital learners prefer to access information quickly from multiple-media sources, but many educators prefer slow and controlled release of information from limited sources.
- Digital learners prefer parallel processing and multitasking, but many educators prefer linear processing and single tasks or limited multitasking.
- Digital learners prefer random access to hyper-linked multimedia information, but many educators prefer to provide information linearly, logically, and sequentially.
- Digital learners prefer to learn "just in time," but many educators prefer to teach "just in case."
- Digital learners prefer instant gratification and immediate rewards, but many educators prefer deferred gratification and delayed rewards.
- Digital learners prefer to network simultaneously with others, but many educators prefer students to work independently before they network and interact.
- Digital learners prefer processing pictures, sounds, color, and video before text, but many educators prefer to provide text before picture, sound, and video.
- Digital learners prefer learning that is relevant, active, instantly useful, and fun, but many educators feel compelled to teach memorization of the content in the curriculum guide.

The learners that we now embrace in our schools grew up with laptops instead of books. They use keyboards more than they do pens. Students today want to know things all of the time. In their world, they can use numerous digital tools to learn whatever they want, any time and from anywhere. These students have been raised in a technology-rich environment, accept that this environment is the norm, and they have grown up surrounded by digital devices that they regularly use to interact with other people and the outside world (Prensky, 2001). They are what many refer to as Millennials or active learners.

As a result of the growing disconnect between their world and the world where they are supposed to receive a formal education, many students are bored with the classroom. The environment outside of school is more engaging, relevant, and meaningful. They routinely communicate with friends, see faces, hear voices, create works of art, and engage in conversations with other learners on the other side of the school world. *Their* world is drastically different from that of the schools they attend and the educators tasked with teaching them. The active learner often seeks knowledge online rather than using a textbook and has little tolerance for delays. This makes it important for educators to provide feedback to their queries. For many active learners, the idea of constructing knowledge within a social community has a great deal of appeal (Skiba & Baron, 2006).

Society has created these active learners that schools need to keep up with, not the other way around. They crave choices and want to be connected. Their connections mean everything. When they discover something they like, they are excited to share it with their friends using digital devices and social media tools. This is how they want their educational experience to be. Active learners want to learn collaboratively and to apply what they have learned through creative pathways. They prefer learning on their own time and on their own terms and want to be involved in real-life issues that matter to them. They want to use their personal devices to take notes or, better yet, take pictures of teacher notes using a cell phone. At New Milford High School in New Jersey, this has become widely accepted by both students and teachers. The traditional way of doing things does not have the same impact it once did. Educators need to think about our own behaviors in the digital age and work to apply them for the betterment of learners of all ages.

It is important to understand that, even though today's active learners have grown up with technology, it does not always follow that they know how to use it effectively for learning. This is the responsibility of schools. We are tasked with preparing students for success in a world that is becoming more dependent on technology, a world that is also in need of a workforce that can think critically, solve real-world problems, and function entrepreneurially.

SUMMARY

Leaders need to be aware of the changing educational landscape, which includes societal shifts in technology use, advances in educational technology, and a new type of learner. Acknowledging and beginning to understand these changes are the first steps to developing a vision and strategic plan for creating a learning culture that provides access to tools that foster essential skill sets, celebrates success, supports innovation, and inspires students to learn and ultimately achieve. Digital leadership can begin here. If we discount the shifts occurring outside our walls and fail to embrace the new type of learner coming into our buildings, we will never develop the capacity to anticipate needed changes that will transform school culture for the better.

2

Why Schools Must Change

"Those who work in a school system are the victims of TTWWADI—That's The Way We've Always Done It. Schools have operated this way for such a long time that most people who work there don't really know the reasons why they do the things they do."

—Kelly, McCain, and Jukes (2009)

During the nineteenth century, there was a dire need to prepare students for assimilation into a workforce in response to the rapid increase in manufacturing. As our nation and the world became industrialized, school became the central institution to provide students with the skills to succeed in this new work environment, which aligned itself to the pressing needs of manufacturing. As these organizations evolved and competition increased, the need for workers who were more efficient and possessed specialized skill sets also increased. As the twentieth century approached, innovation continued to have a profound impact on formal schooling. The increased efficiency and productivity of Henry Ford's assembly line trickled down and eventually impacted school structure and function. For all intents and purposes, schools modelled themselves after these assembly lines, and teachers became specialized to teach only one general subject throughout the school day. A school's *raison d'être* became that of organizing students into distinct roles in order to prepare them for the various industry-specific jobs that awaited them. America's system of education changed forever, and schools mirrored the assembly lines where many of its graduates would end up. Curricula leaned heavily on the memorization of facts, and the skills taught were those that were pivotal to success in the industrial age.

Obviously, many things began to change as technology become more advanced, requiring a different type of workforce with skills that exceeded those needed in manufacturing. The transition from agriculture to manufacturing eventually gave way to a variety of new occupations in service, professional, and technical areas; thus, more and more students began to seek additional education upon graduating from high school. The need for a bachelor's degree became a prerequisite for a job. This soon changed to the requirement of a master's degree in many professions as society moved from an industrialized to a globalized economy. Despite these major changes over the years, one thing remained unchanged: the structure of schools.

If you walk into any secondary school building in this country, chances are it will eerily resemble any other one you've seen. The day will be structured into periods, and bells will signify movement from one class to the next. Students will have a different teacher for each subject as well as a textbook or workbook. Each room will have desks aligned in rows where students will obediently take notes, answer questions, and complete either group or individual work. Lectures or other direct forms of content delivery will dominate class time. The day typically ends with the assignment of homework in some or all of the classes. After everything is said and done, all of the students will be assessed using either standardized methods or internally generated tools chock-full of fill-in-the-blank and multiple choice questions. In this way, public education has become nothing more than a cog factory, churning out workers that can be successful in a factory or consumers that will purchase what is being produced (Godin, 2010). Is this what your school looks like? More important, is this what the real world looks like?

Standardization and the current reform movement heavily dependent on high-stakes testing are further reducing the education system to a model that does not work for our students. Students are not motivated by standardized tests, as they find no true meaning and value in them. Teachers can become motivated for all the wrong reasons, including job security or financial incentives. A focus on standardization narrows the curriculum and creates a teaching culture where creativity, exploration, and critical thinking are scarce or nonexistent. It creates a culture that students distain; one that can only be sustained with the use of "if-then" rewards or "carrots and sticks." There has to be a better direction. If schools continue down the same course, they risk inhibiting creativity and reinforcing an outdated model that will not prepare our students for their future.

Standardization continues to follow in the footsteps of the century-old model of education that is focused on industrialization. Such a model stifles the growth of teachers, students, and administrators. This entrenched system produces students who lack creativity, are fearful of failure, work extremely hard to follow directions (do homework, study for tests, not question authority), and are leaving schools with obsolete skills in a postindustrial society. Schools focus more on filling the minds of students with useless facts and knowledge than giving them essential skills that can't be measured with a #2 pencil.

As noted in Chapter 1, the world we live in has fundamentally changed. Learners have transitioned to the Information Age while schools continue to operate under the constructs, ideas, and assumptions of the industrial age (Kelly et al., 2009). The conundrum is that we want our students to be prepared for whatever the future holds for them. Life will be dramatically different for our learners in the near and far future, given the pace of change in a technologically driven world, but our current education system does not adequately prepare them for the kinds of jobs and challenges they are likely to encounter in their lifetimes (Schrum & Levin, 2009). Kelly et al. (2009, p. 9) note the fundamental disconnect between students and the schools they attend:

- The industrial efficiency model envisioned for teaching in the early twentieth century is not reflected in learning efficiency for students in the twenty-first century.
- The learning styles of today's digital learners are significantly different than those for whom our schools were originally designed, especially high schools. They work, think, and learn differently—and our schools are not designed for them.
- Instruction is primarily based on teachers talking in classrooms, textbooks, memorization, and content-based tests; as such, schools are out of sync with the world around them.
- Schools focus on linear, sequential, left-brain thinking in a world that requires both left- and right-brain capabilities.
- The segregation of skills and tasks that typified the industrial approach is reflected today in our approach to creating schools for the future—and it does not serve us well.

Everything is changing—society, the educational landscape, and learners—and it is time for educational leaders to embody a modern, progressive form of leadership. More often than not, the individuals trusted with leading change in the twenty-first century are the least knowledgeable about the twenty-first century. Education is at a crossroads, and it needs innovative leaders who possess the knowledge, skills, and fortitude to move schools forward. We can no longer sit back and watch our schools become less and less relevant while failing to meet the needs of our learners and other stakeholders. The actions of school leaders will ultimately determine the fate of schools as we continue to advance further into the twenty-first century. Digital leadership is about establishing a vision and implementing a strategic process that creates a teaching and learning culture that provides students with essential skill sets: creativity, communication, collaboration, critical thinking, problem solving, technological proficiency, and global awareness. It is also about how each of us approaches our work through the lens of these skill sets that will redefine not only the structure of schools, but also our capacity to lead and initiate sustainable change. Digital leadership focuses on a consistent pursuit of innovation, effective integration of technology, quality professional development, transparency, celebration of successes from which others may learn, establishment of relationships with stakeholders, an open mind, and anticipation of continued change. It flies in the face of TTWWADI and allows us to reinvent education.

This imperative has become more difficult because of budget cuts and what seems like a relentless attack on the profession of education, which have taken their toll on staff morale. Digital leadership thus becomes even more essential for cultivating a school culture whose primary focus is on the learning and achievement of each and every student.

A SCHOOL LEADER'S CALL TO ARMS

Architect Louis Sullivan once said, "Form ever follows function." In no place has that precept ever been truer than in our schools, from cafeterias to classrooms. Yesterday's students, often destined for the factory floor or service work, attended schools functionally designed to teach institutional compliance. In the 1990s, America outsourced its factories; yet today's factory schools continue to warehouse young people, despite the fact that America no longer needs a workforce trained for the last century. This is why Dr. Pam Moran's district embarked ten years ago on significant changes in their work to optimize learning among young people for this century. Pam has worked in the Albemarle School District adjacent to Charlottesville, Virginia, since 1986, and has been its superintendent for the past eight years. She was the first female superintendent in the district (Moran, 2013).

It seems like Pam is on to something. Schools in her county were preparing students for a world that no longer existed. The National Academies Press emphasizes the way in which schools should be structured in its recent publication, *Education for Life and Work: Developing Transferable Knowledge and Skills in the 21st Century*, which aligns with Pam's push for change:

> When the goal is to prepare students to be successful in solving new problems and adapting to new situations, then deeper learning is called for. Calls for such 21st century skills as innovation, creativity, and creative problem-solving can also be seen as calls for deeper learning—helping students develop transferable knowledge that can be applied to solve new problems or respond effectively to new situations. (National Research Council, 2012, p. 70)

As noted in Chapter 1, current learners inhabit a world in which multimodal communication, face-to-face and virtual teamwork, self-initiated problem solving, and creative solution finding have fast become the normative expectation, not the exception, at work, in homes, and across communities. Young people don't depend on home editions of *World Book*, the library, or their teachers for information or "do-it-yourself" solutions (Riedel, 2012). They go straight to Wikipedia, YouTube, Twitter, and Facebook—or they text a friend. With the rapid acceleration of new technologies, the world has changed for these neomillennials' grandparents and their parents, but the schools that they, themselves, attend haven't evolved much at all.

Young people still often languish in mass-standardized schools where desks in rows, the dominant teaching wall, print on paper, one-size-fits-all testing, bell schedules, and an outright focus on compliance are key to controlling and limiting learners' work. Frederick Taylor's "cult of efficiency," essential to assembly lines, piecework, and repetitive processes of the factory floor, remains well established inside schools, regardless of the build date. This is not true of other professions.

Over time, the practices, tools, and work spaces of physicians have changed to reflect contemporary research and new technologies to better serve patients. Lawyers use online research resources to prepare briefs and contractual agreements on behalf of clients. Automotive technicians download data from vehicles to determine what repairs and maintenance are needed. Big box stores have automated the supply chain to monitor and replenish inventory as sales occur. Even trash trucks and taxis have Quick Response (QR) codes affixed to them to lead potential customers to their websites. Every sector, every job, every employee today has had to respond to twenty-first-century changes, often because of new technologies. A recent headline in *The New York Times* that profiled one of the critical changes in the for-profit sector read: "To Stay Relevant in a Career, Workers Train Nonstop" (Dewan, 2012).

Educators Pam works with in her district have sought to understand the dynamic of global changes that young people will face in their future. They've asked, "Isn't it past time for education and educators to respond to twenty-first century changes as well? Isn't it time to move from teaching places limited by the walls of classrooms and schools to learning spaces, limitless in possibilities, that extend educational opportunities beyond school walls and district boundaries? Isn't it time to stop paying attention to political and private sector agendas that promote twentieth century standardization methodologies and, instead, attend to the need to 'destandardize' curricula, assessment, and pedagogy so we can get to unlimited, deep learning?"

Today, when she walks through schools inside or outside her own district, Pam looks at how staff reconfigure their use of space so that learners can work privately or together in larger or smaller groups and teams, and with a choice of tools, both virtually through the Internet and face to face. The concept of space, both physical and virtual, provides a critical entry point for instructional change to occur so that educators can personalize, individualize, and differentiate learning through the use of new technologies. Creative flexibility and the adaptability of space in schools serve as starting points for students to produce what they learn, not just consume what an adult teaches. Space matters. Tech matters. According to Pam, though, it is our teachers who remain the determining factors in whether learning will be transformed to represent what young people need for today and tomorrow, not for yesterday's world.

Recently, she visited a new school outside of her district that was built as a series of interactive learning spaces—a school for the twenty-first century, not the twentieth. Its design would serve any level of school, elementary to high. She was part of a small group inspecting this "best-in-class" school, which was constructed to reflect advances in neuroscience and educational design research that teach us that learners benefit from fresh air, movement, and natural light in a learning environment. It was a school built for project-based learning. Pam wanted to experience a school designed from the ground up with twenty-first-century learning at its core, because her district is similarly committed to transforming pedagogy, resources, and learning spaces.

Created with experiential learning in mind, the airy spaces in this school were designed so that active learners could collaborate, create, and share. Faceted light tubes brighten hallways and the gym with natural light on days when winter clouds darken the morning sky. Window seating, wide enough for two or more children to curl up with a good paper or e-book, punctuates swaths of glass that stretch across outer classroom walls. The art room and library open onto spacious decks designed to entice learners into open air. In addition to integration of a food lab, a learning lounge, state-of-the-art composting facilities, a "teaching kitchen," and a performance area that opens into the dining space, cafeteria doors lead to large raised-bed vegetable gardens irrigated from a rainwater harvesting and collection system.

A combination of open and closed flexible learning spaces link nooks and open areas—labeled "nest," "canopy," "cave," and "woodlands"—to natural environments outside the school. Furniture and technology tools afford a continuum of choices and zones of comfort for learners and educators alike. It was what many educators would characterize as a "dream" of a school.

Despite these innovations, Pam found that teachers and children were not doing the work she had anticipated. A teacher commented to her openly, "I'd prefer desks with built-in storage areas for textbooks. When the kids need to go get their social studies texts, it takes ten minutes out of the block." Pam watched learners complete worksheet after worksheet, read in "round-robin" style, and listen to teacher-directed instruction. The message—whether posted as reading rules, library rules, or class rules—was, in essence, "Be compliant. Sit down. Be silent." Whiteboard and other technologies lay mostly unused, expensive devices lost to learning.

In a school filled with state-of-the-art learning spaces, tools, and resources, students' work mirrored the traditions of a twentieth-century education. Despite the innovative space design and tools present in this school for the future, it was still a teaching place of the past. On the surface everything had changed, yet in the reality of learners, nothing had really evolved.

The district had invested significant resources in advanced technologies and learning spaces. Some would say there should be no barriers to contemporary learning in this new school. Yet little pedagogical change was evident in either the use of new spaces or technologies.

For Pam, the situation begs the question, Why do some educators, in her own district and beyond, resist change, particularly, in the face of the significant shifts occurring around us in the world? Is it that we do not notice the shifts or that we see them as irrelevant to our own work? Perhaps we do not know what we need to do differently or why we need to change anyway. Could it be that we simply resist change because of our own fears of failure? Is it because of the standardization movement that's embedded in schools everywhere? Or, in the best tradition of the iconic multiple-choice test, is it all of the above?

She has discussed with her school board and staff how traditional trends of education represent the same multiple governmental failures identified by the 911 Commission: failure of policy, management, organizational capacity, and imagination. In the education sector in general, we build policy based on old paradigms, still work mostly in silos, lack strategies to build consistent capacity to use new pedagogies and tools, and fail to imagine a future that will be substantively different than yesterday or even today. Pam believes that as leaders, we must question at every opportunity our commitment to sustaining practices that need to be abandoned for the sake of contemporary learners.

Moore's Law represents a norm in our world—that is, there will continue to be rapid shifts in the evolution and extinction of technologies in the workforce, our personal lives, and our social communities. People go to work today, not in cubicles or on assembly lines, but in their own homes and highly active spaces in which technologies seamlessly blend into jobs—whether at McDonald's, Google, or an automotive repair shop. A recent visit to an advanced manufacturing "collaboratory" at the University of Virginia provided Pam with a glimpse of contemporary engineering work areas: a multipurpose space that combined lounge seating with programming and design space, partitioned only by a glass wall from a construction laboratory filled with 3-D printers and test spaces. The chair of the department explained that classical engineering curricula, like today's medical school curricula, is evolving from disciplines taught in isolation to transdisciplinary learning, and that the field of engineering no longer operates singularly, but as one in which engineers must draw from multiple fields to design, engineer, test, and manufacture.

This kind of change is everywhere in the workforce. However, change being advanced in our district isn't *just* about the workforce. It's also about how humans search, connect, communicate, and create as members of a global community, and within our own families. It's about citizenship, including digital citizenship. If we expect learners to continue to evolve in their experiences with us and throughout their lives, why would we not expect them to power up their learning in our schools with contemporary tools to connect with peers and experts across our schools, districts, the nation, and the globe?

People live today, as Google's Pascal Finette (2012) says, in "a culture of participation plus technologies plus networks" that will, in his opinion, change the course of human history. Last spring, high school seniors in Pam's district conversed via Skype with an Egyptologist who was boots-on-the-ground in the revolutionary streets of Cairo. Their connection? A student teacher with family in Egypt. Kindergarten children in two different schools recently explored *J* words in a lesson cotaught by their teachers and an educator from Michigan—via their class Twitter account. Pam has been invited to comment on first- and third-graders' blogs. She has watched from her couch the live broadcast of three schools' winter orchestra concerts via Ustream and observed sixth graders characterizing contemporary lyrics as poetry in their own virtual, multimedia "op-ed" posts. She has visited multiage Coder Dojos (available at k12albemarlesupt.wordpress.com/2012/10/02/learning-about-scratch-by-eileen/), where students, age six to eighteen, informally learn from and with one another and teachers to use multiple programming tools.

Pam believes that students in our nation's schools are winners or losers depending on whether they are the recipients of annual random acts of excellence or not. A learner can end up in a state-of-the art-school facility where pedagogy still remains command and control, driven by a "one-to-some" teaching model through curricula, assessment, and instructional standardization minimize opportunities for young people to pursue interests, passions, and possibilities. Or a child can enter a school district or class where he or she is afforded opportunities that evoke passion, capability, resiliency, and self-direction. In such learning spaces where questions, curiosity, and risk taking are nurtured, young people don't "power down" their tools or their minds when they cross the threshold of school. Instead, they learn today what they need for today—and tomorrow. That's what she believes every young person deserves in her district.

The Albemarle County Schools recognize that deep, necessary change does not come from changing spaces, tools, or other resources alone. It comes from supporting professionals to invest in studying, connecting, communicating, and learning together, beginning with their own questions, curiosity, and interests as learners. We expect young people, regardless of whether they attend a school built in the 1930s or one built in the twenty-first century, to acquire lifelong learning competencies that transcend the knowledge they need today, knowing it will be different tomorrow.

The deep changes Pam observes have come from ten years of ongoing professional work by teachers, principals, and central staff—educators working together in vertical and horizontal learning communities and leadership teams. Each summer they have come together to study, plan, and develop curricula that are concept centered and standards aligned. They have taken time to identify, use, and evolve instructional practices that are personalized, differentiated, and individualized to how young people learn. In the most recent iteration of their work, teachers have created open and interdisciplinary performance tasks designed to inform assessments in an effort to move beyond standardized testing as the measure of success.

Is everyone on board in Pam's district with the changes being made? Absolutely not. However, the ethos and culture of learning communities continue to shift among its educators, who are more tuned in than ever to considering and answering the question, "Why change?"

THE TIME FOR EXCUSES IS OVER

We can no longer afford to sustain a school structure built for a time long past. What will it take for the lightbulb to finally go on and the long, difficult process of change to begin? Success in this endeavor relies on us to take a no-excuse attitude. Ask yourself this: What am I prepared to do to improve all facets of my school? How will I accomplish more with less? Leaders must think and reflect upon the ways to accomplish established goals as opposed to worrying about the challenges, roadblocks, and pushback that one will surely experience. These are all common complications that arise during the change process and should not be excuses not to push forward.

Leaders must be the pillars of their respective institutions and focus on solutions rather than problems. Succumbing to the negative rhetoric, abiding by the status quo, and having a bunker mentality will do nothing to initiate needed changes in buildings to improve teaching and learning. Each day leaders are afforded an opportunity to make a positive difference in the lives of students. One's passion for helping all students learn and desire to assist staff in their growth should be the driving motivational forces to make schools the best they can be, regardless of the obstacles.

As noted in Chapter 1, everything is changing—the world, learners, the job market, technology, access to information—yet the sad reality is that schools are not. Digital leadership emphasizes the need for current leaders to be catalysts to drive sustainable change that will transform school culture. Only then will schools produce learners ready to take on the world and able to succeed in a demanding society ever more reliant on digital fluency and an entrepreneurial thought process. Leaders must begin to map out collective responses that focus on positive solutions to the problems inherent in school culture.

MODEL A VISION FOR EXCELLENCE, INNOVATION, AND CREATIVITY

Jobs available today have changed radically due to the rise of globalization, the continuous surge of outsourcing by many businesses and industries, increasing immigration, and a flattened world (Friedman, 2005). Schools need to change in the face of this challenge if they are to create the next generation of entrepreneurs, scientists, politicians, and engineers who work in a technology-rich and technology-driven world. With this modern workforce as the goal, what do we want our schools to look like? Why do we need to change? Are we doing what's best to meet the needs of our learners who have grown up in the digital age with ubiquitous access to information? Leaders must begin by articulating a clear vision to their staff that, if we are to change, we must be willing to shed some strongly embedded ideals, opinions, and behaviors that have shaped our schools for over a century. The consensus has to be that every student can and should learn, and that educators must learn how to push us to become ever better. Getting your entire staff to embrace these concepts is at the heart of digital leadership. I prefer to use the word *embrace* rather than *buy-in*, a more commonly used word synonymous with change efforts. We should not be trying to "sell" our staffs on pedagogical techniques and other initiatives that will better prepare our students for success in today's constantly evolving society once they graduate. The envisioning and resulting strategic planning process need to address the interconnected questions of *why, what, where,* and *how* in this order (Jones, 2008):

- *Why* involves convincing all stakeholders why a school needs to change.
- *What* is the content of the change, built through a common focus. It involves using good data, research, and best practices to determine what needs to change once people understand why.
- *Where* defines the location and direction, which involves assessing the present status, agreeing on a common direction, and defining ways to measure improvement in student achievement. In the case of digital leadership, it also must define ways to measure improvement in professional learning, communications, and public relations.
- *How* is the process of change and involves determining how to change the school once people understand and embrace the *why, what,* and *where.*

An honest dialogue centering on these questions will provide a rationale and direction for why the school or leader must change. In order to promote the embracement of new ideas, strategies, and techniques, we need to collaboratively work with staff to transform traditional classroom environments into vibrant learning communities where all students are authentically engaged. Consistently engaging staff in brainstorming sessions in order to develop a collective vision on how to transform the school for the betterment of all students should be a routine practice.

EMBRACE TWENTY-FIRST-CENTURY PEDAGOGY, CURRICULUM, AND INSTRUCTION

A vision begins with talk, but it will only become reality with action. As society evolves due to advances in technology, we as digital leaders, must ensure that instruction, learning, and other leadership functions follow suit or we run the risk of our schools becoming irrelevant. By irrelevant I am referring to our ability to prepare students with the skills to think critically, solve problems, demonstrate learning through creation, and compete in a global society. How well we model these essential skills goes a long way in changing attitudes, beliefs, and behaviors.

As instructional leaders, it is our primary responsibility to observe and evaluate instruction. With this comes the responsibility to ensure that teachers are provided the freedom to take risks, knowledge of effective practices, resources to make it happen, and flexibility to incorporate innovative teaching strategies. With these parameters in place, leaders must then be able to consistently identify, foster, support, and promote twenty-first-century pedagogy. An easy way to ensure this is to incorporate the four Cs—*creativity, communication, critical thinking*, and *collaboration*—into curriculum and lesson design.

Inherent within this shift is the need to reevaluate the curriculum and pedagogy as the real-time Web and Information Age present new challenges to instruction and student engagement. The time is now for us to lay the foundation to ensure that our students evolve into critical consumers of

Figure 2.1   Pedagogical Framework for the Twenty-First Century

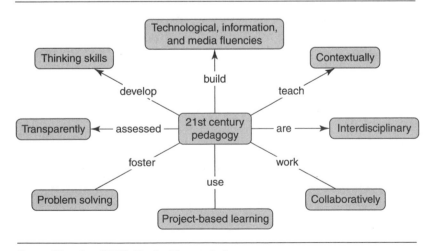

Source: Churches (2008). Used with premission.

content; understand the importance of digital citizenship; and possess the ability to create, analyze, and interpret an array of media messages. Leaders have to make concerted efforts to see where educational technology aligns well to the curriculum and pedagogy. Chapter 1 presented a snapshot of the many tools and resources available to schools today that can assist with the transformation in this area. With all of the choices available today, as well as the relentless marketing campaigns by educational technology companies, it is easy to succumb to making rash decisions. Leaders must be cognizant of this and ask themselves what they want students and teachers to do with these tools to enhance learning instead of what do they want to buy. Twenty-first-century pedagogy, curriculum, and instruction rely on leaders taking the time to evaluate technology to justify its expense while ensuring that it will have a positive impact on learning. The U.S. Department of Education (2012) through the Office of Educational Technology published the report *Expanding Evidence Approaches for Learning in a Digital World,* which calls for smart change by presenting educators, policymakers, and funders with an expanded view of evidence approaches and sources of data that can help them with decision making about learning resources. Leaders can now refer to this comprehensive resource to determine which products and approaches make the best investment that will support student learning. The report can be downloaded at www .ed.gov/edblogs/technology/evidence-framework/. Begin by gathering key stakeholders to review this report and collaboratively revise your curriculum to incorporate the right technology to emphasize essential skills necessary for today's learners to excel beyond the building walls.

Focus on Bold Ideas

All around the world, there are ideas that are put into action. These ideas, for the most part, put student learning front and center and consist of experiences that enhance essential skills.

These include creativity, problem solving, critical thinking, technological proficiency, global awareness, media literacy, communication, and collaboration. These skills lead to the promotion of ingenuity, entrepreneurialism, and self-directed learning. The majority of schools in the United States do not place a high value on this type of learning. Current reform practices and a system of education still entrenched in preparing students for an industrialized society extinguish many schools' attempts at embracing a better way of learning. One of the culprits is a mentality of incrementalism, in which leaders make small changes in existing policies or procedures rather than radical innovations. It is no secret that the process of making changes is fraught with issue after issue. Most are content with the way things are, and anything more than a small change presents a challenge to the status quo. This is, after all, what we hear and experience from those who resist change.

As leaders, it is our duty to be agents of change. We must collaboratively develop and implement our own bold ideas to improve the learning process in a way that emphasizes our students' cognitive growth, passions, and strengths, while challenging them to push their own boundaries. It is difficult work to transform a culture of learning that has been embedded for nearly a century, but every problem in education has been solved sometime or somewhere before. Now is the time for all of us to critically analyze our respective schools and take a stand against the status quo in order to do what is best for our students.

The best ideas in the world don't succumb to incrementalism or any other type of excuse or challenge (Stager, 2005). Bold ideas revolve around respecting the learning, authentic problems, real tools and materials, expanded learning opportunities, collegiality, and lessons from outside of education.

Respect for Each Learner

Respect for each learner is pivotal if leaders want to create schools where digital tools are used responsibly and routinely.

We need to have actual conversations with our students. Respecting students means regarding them with special attention, honoring them, showing consideration toward them, being concerned about them, appreciating them, relating to them, admiring their strengths, and caring for them (Tomlinson, 2011). They must be part of the transformation efforts, and their voices can provide invaluable feedback in efforts to reshape everything from curriculum, to pedagogy, to technology purchases, to how time for learning is allocated. Respect also entails consistently seeking paths to grow professionally in order to discover and implement new ideas on their behalf.

Authentic Problems

Authentic problems provide a meaningful and relevant context for learning. This is as "real world" as it gets. Through problem-based learning, students learn how to use an iterative process of assessing what they know, identifying what they need to know, gathering information, and collaborating on the evaluation of hypotheses in light of the data they have collected (Stepien & Gallagher, 1993). In addition to a focus on a real-world problem that mimics the work of professionals, authentic learning involves a presentation of findings to audiences beyond the classroom; engages students in discourse and social learning in a community of learners; has students direct their own learning in project work; and actively uses open-ended inquiry, thinking skills, and metacognition (Rule, 2006). This type of learning can be messy and unstructured at times, which is why solid leadership is needed to embed it as an embraced pedagogical technique that is employed regularly, not sparingly. In my opinion, there is no more powerful learning strategy than to have students exposed to and tackle problems that have meaning and relevancy.

Students are using technology to solve problems outside of school. They are also creating their own technology in some cases. Learners are capable of incredible things if they are placed in the right environment and afforded the opportunity to use real tools and materials. It is our responsibility to create these environments. To do so, we must relinquish control, provide support (i.e., purchasing the right tools and providing quality professional development), encourage calculated risk taking, exhibit flexibility, and model expectations.

Expanded Opportunities

The adoption of the Common Core Standards has placed pressure on schools to ensure that students are college and career ready upon graduation. A curriculum, instructional strategies, and assessments aligned to the Common Core Standards can only go so far in preparing students for the rigors they will experience either in college or careers. Expanded opportunities that serve as an extension to the curriculum have the potential to greatly increase a student's readiness as defined by the Common Core Standards. We have made great strides in this area in my district through the development of the Academies at New Milford High School. Through this initiative, all students have the opportunity to be exposed to authentic learning experiences, online courses, specialized field trips, independent study, credit for learning experiences outside of school, and internships. We plan eventually to incorporate capstone projects into our Academies program as well. More detail on this will be presented in Chapter 11.

Collegiality and Collaboration

Let's face it, as educators, we need to work together in order to successfully implement the best ideas to improve teaching and learning. We must overcome personal agendas, bring the naysayers on board, implement a system focused on shared decision making, and move to initiate a change process that is sustainable. The best ideas will only become realities through collegiality and collaboration.

Lessons From Outside Education

Some of the best ideas for why schools need to change and how to go about it come from outside the field of education. In *Linchpin*, Seth Godin (2010) writes,

> Every day I meet people who have so much to give but have been bullied enough or frightened enough to hold it back. It's time to stop complying with the system and draw your own map. You have brilliance in you, your contribution is essential, and the art you create is precious. Only you can do it, and you must.

Godin's work focuses on the concept of a linchpin, the essential building block of great organizations. To Godin, linchpins are indispensable, love their work, understand that there is no playbook, and challenge the status quo. Every day, linchpins set out to turn each day into a work of art. Creating a school and culture that parallel the real world is, in itself, a work of art. Linchpin leaders, although not entirely indispensable, are creative, see or are able to discover solutions to issues, develop strong connections with a variety of stakeholder groups, and help others solve problems. Digital leadership is about inspiring students and teachers to think rather than follow rulebooks and ace tests. It is about making a profound difference, and it begins with acknowledging the shortcomings of the system, building a plan to lead schools differently in the digital age, and then doing something about it.

In *Drive*, Daniel Pink (2011) takes a look at what truly motivates us based on scientific research. Drawing on four decades of research, he reveals society's need to use a carrot-and-stick approach or an if-then rewards system as the means to extrinsically reward people for the work they do. Our educational system is brimming with extrinsic rewards, and the latest example, merit pay, could be the worst idea yet. As Pink discovered, a carrot-and-stick approach worked well in the twentieth century, just like the industrialized education model worked well for creating the workforce needed, but it does not work well for the creative work that is now in demand in schools or the real world.

It definitely does not work well for leaders interested in change. Extrinsic motivational forces crowd out good behavior, diminish performance, crush creativity, encourage shortcuts or unethical behavior, foster short-term thinking, and essentially eliminate intrinsic motivation. "Carrots and sticks are so last century. For 21st century work, we need to upgrade to autonomy, mastery and purpose" (Pink, 2011, p. 203). For schools to change, leaders must work on creating cultures that focus on intrinsic means of motivation driven by autonomy, mastery, and purpose. Autonomy is the desire to direct our own lives. Mastery is the urge to get better and better at something that matters. Purpose is the yearning to do what we do in the service of something larger than ourselves.

Google understands the importance of fostering a climate fueled by intrinsic motivation. As a result, the company has developed an 80/20 innovation time-off model (ITO) where 80% of employee time is spent on core projects and about 20% is spent on activities of personal interest that will ultimately impact Google's bottom line. Google recognized that relinquishing control and unleashing creativity were the keys to innovation and change. This model also fits in nicely with the elements of intrinsic motivation identified by Pink. Imagine a school where teachers could spend time working on projects that they own, that could make them think differently and passionately about their work during the other 80% of their time?

Digital leadership focuses on fostering intrinsic motivation as the primary catalyst for change. It is about developing our own innovation policies to initiate meaningful change. As a leader, this is the type of teaching and learning culture that we should want to foster and cultivate, one where creativity flourishes, students find relevancy and meaning in their learning, and teachers are given the support and autonomy to be innovative. Think about how you can apply the concepts of autonomy, mastery, and purpose to your work and that of your students and staff. Chapter 8 will highlight how New Milford High School, New Jersey, incorporated the 80/20 ITO model as an intrinsic innovative force to change instruction based upon teacher interests, not those dictated from the top down.

Every child can learn, regardless of his or her innate level of intelligence, and gaps in achievement can be mitigated through research and understanding of differences in individual background and opportunity (Glazer, 2009). This also holds true for leaders as well. In *Outliers*, Malcolm Gladwell (2008) takes a detailed look at the characteristics and secrets of successful people. He defines an outlier as a person who, for one reason or another, is so accomplished and so extraordinary and so outside of ordinary experience that he or she is puzzling to the rest of us.

A great deal can be learned from Gladwell and applied to educational leadership. Successful leaders are not necessarily those with the highest IQs. Instead, they are those who are "smart enough" to recognize and take advantage of the unique opportunities that present themselves. Digital leadership is about discovering, recognizing, and taking advantage of the many opportunities that the digital age presents. This represents an entirely different construct as it breaks away from the mold associated with traditional leadership. It is about seizing the opportunity to pursue any possible learning path or area of interest to improve the schools we work in and ourselves.

If we think about the outlier not as a leader who falls beyond the normal boundaries of the education system, but rather as someone whose leadership makes them fall beyond society's expectations of what an educational leader looks like, everything falls into place. Leaders who position themselves to be outliers are, in a natural way, facilitating the type of innovative and creative thinking that is necessary to thrive in an information-based economy. Isn't this what our schools need? In a world where the creation and dissemination of new information is the key to economic viability, leaders today actually have to be outliers to some extent in order to initiate and sustain the type of change needed in our schools, especially those schools still functioning to prepare learners for an industrialized workforce and as a result have become unaligned with society. The very nature of the Internet and the vast and constantly changing educational opportunities available on it need to be harnessed by leaders for their own development and that of their schools. Those who recognize and act on this will ultimately become outliers as the resulting changes create a paradigm shift in leadership style as well as school structure and function.

Become a Technology Leader

Technology is not going away, and leaders, regardless of their experience, need to understand this. For schools truly to be relevant, meaningful centers for learning in today's digital age, it will take leaders who are not afraid to go beyond their comfort zones to lead. Many of the changes schools need are dependent on the ability and desire of leaders to hone specific skills, behaviors, and characteristics associated with technology. The National Association of Secondary School Principals (NASSP) identified the following ten guidelines to assist school leaders in integrating technology in their schools and leadership practices (Demsky, 2012):

- Principals must effectively and consistently model the use of the same technology tools they expect teachers to use in their classrooms with the students.
- Principals must be consistent in their decisions and expectations about integrating learning technology in the school.
- The principal's communication about the pace and process of integrating learning technology needs to be clear and reasonable.
- The principal must provide appropriate professional development time and resources to support effective classroom implementation of technology.

- The principal must support early adopters and risk takers.
- The principal must do whatever it takes to ensure that all staff has early access to the very same digital tools that students will be using in their classrooms.
- As the educational leader, the principal must make it clear to the technology leader that all decisions relating to learning technology will be made by the educational leaders with input from the technology leaders, not the other way around.
- The principal must set and support the expectation that student work will be done and stored using technology.
- Principals must ensure that families and the public are kept informed about the school's goals and progress relating to its use of technology as a learning resource.
- The principal must be an active and public champion for all students, staff members, and the school of implementing a vision of fully integrating learning technology for the second decade of the twenty-first century.

Leaders need to understand the true value of technology. In October of 2012, my family suffered a devastating loss as my grandmother passed away only a few weeks after being diagnosed with a malignant brain tumor. Abiding by her wishes not to inconvenience anyone, my parents arranged for friends and family to call an hour prior to the funeral, which was then followed by a short service. Because the funeral was held just days after her death, her two sisters were not able to physically attend the service in New Jersey. One of my great aunts resides in rural Arkansas, while the other lives in Texas.

My wife's family was heartbroken that they were not able to attend the service, as were both of my great aunts. The night before the service, we called the funeral home to see if it had the capability of streaming the service over the Internet. This would have enabled family that could not be there to view the service. Unfortunately, we were informed that, although the funeral home was currently working on setting up this service, it would not be operational in time for us to use it. Even after receiving this news, I still took my Mac Book Pro with me to the funeral home. At this time I still do not know why, since I was told that there was no Internet connection available.

I arrived early on the morning of the service, and on a wing and a prayer, I booted up my computer to find that there was a strong Wi-Fi signal that I could utilize. At this point, I created a free Ustream account in a matter of seconds, as I had heard about this service through many of the connected educators that I communicate with on a regular basis. After creating this free account, my brother contacted my great aunt in Arkansas and we tested out the live stream. To our surprise, it worked! The computer was left unattended to stream my grandmother's funeral service live to her sister in Arkansas while we mourned and took part in the service. She was able to watch the entire service uninterrupted. Afterward, she sent me an e-mail that brought me to tears as she expressed the priceless moment that I was able to provide her. A few days later, my grandmother's other sister watched the archived recording of the service. None of this would have been possible without technology.

That night, I returned home, as I was hosting the third annual Edscape Conference at my school. It was a bittersweet moment for me, as I was still grieving the loss of my grandmother, but I was excited to welcome 350 educators from ten states and Canada to my school. Using the knowledge I gained the day before, I was determined to try to establish a live feed of the keynote address as well as some of the sessions. Not only was I able to use Ustream and share the keynote address with the world, but I was also able to establish a feed of a presentation by some educators who traveled to New Jersey from Canada so that their superintendent could watch from their province. Again, something like this would not have been possible without technology.

These stories demonstrate the potential that technology has to reshape school cultures and how we learn. Technology is not just a shiny tool that can increase engagement, but a conduit to endless possibilities that can enhance every facet of what we do in education. It is not a frivolous expense that is not worth the investment that many make it out to be. As I demonstrated above, the inherent power of a laptop, Internet connection, webcam, and a free streaming service were able to touch the lives of people a thousand miles away and leave a lasting impact. Imagine what it can do for schools and educators looking to enrich the curriculum while making learning more relevant and meaningful for students. I see technology as a needed resource in education that can break down the walls of traditional school structures while creating new opportunities to learn.

Technology can engage, connect, empower, and enhance teaching, how educators learn, the work done by schools, and stakeholder relations. The driving question we should be asking is how we should use the technology that is available to us to improve what we do instead of why we should use it to improve what we do. Even in schools that might not have many technology resources, time and energy should be spent figuring out how to maximize what is available instead of making endless excuses for not moving forward.

Technology is here to stay, although there is never a shortage of naysayers who question its value. Its value rests in whether leaders decide to use it effectively to positively impact the lives of our students, achieve learning goals, communicate with stakeholders, share best practices, and connect like never before. The results and impact will speak for themselves in ways that standardized tests never could. Is it a silver bullet or a cure for what ails education? Will it eventually replace teachers? Of course not, but one should think twice before claiming that it is not worth the investment. The results of effective integration speak for themselves. Just ask the students, teachers, administrators, parents, and other stakeholders who witness this on a regular basis. Digital leadership relies heavily on technology as a conduit for change.

SUMMARY

The outdated twentieth-century model for education that prepared students for an industrialized workforce no longer fits the needs of society or, more important, that of our learners. Digital leadership is about championing change that will transform schools into vibrant epicenters of learning, like the renaissance led by Dr. Pam Moran in Albemarle County, Virginia. Leaders must critically reflect upon pedagogy, curriculum, learning spaces, and the technological resources that support each of these areas. Once they do, they can begin to create a vision for change that incorporates the big ideas needed to take schools from ambiguity to relevancy. These are the types of schools that will resonate with all stakeholders, set the stage for increases in achievement, and establish a greater sense of pride for the educational work being done.

3

Keys to Leading Sustainable Change

"We must move beyond the implementation phase of change when new ideas and practices are tried for the first time, to the institutionalization phase when new practices are integrated effortlessly into teachers' repertoires. This holds true for leaders as well and might ultimately be more important for sustainable change."

—Anderson and Stiegelbauer (1994)

ONE PRACTITIONER'S JOURNEY

Dr. Spike Cook is the principal of the R. H. Bacon Elementary School in Millville, New Jersey. His story exemplifies how shifting to a new leadership paradigm can initiate change within a school, and eventually a school district, in embracing innovative technological integration strategies. In a relatively short time, Spike became a model for digital leadership by setting the example he wanted to see for his teachers, students, parents, and administrative colleagues. He realized early on in his journey that for change to occur and become sustainable, he needed to establish a vision both for his school and himself as an effective twenty-first-century principal. This required him to take a reflective look at his school's culture in relation to society and anticipate the types of changes that were needed for improvement. He wanted to become a more relevant leader in order to inspire his staff and students to reach their potential.

As part of his 2012 New Year's resolution, Spike began his journey of becoming a connected leader committed to digital leadership principles. He signed up for various social media applications such as Twitter, Google+, and Facebook. Following the lead of other like-minded educators, he launched a blog for himself and his school. In the infancy of his leadership transformation, he followed as many connected principals on Twitter as he could find. He studied the articles they tweeted and how they were representing their schools, and themselves. Many of the examples Spike followed had blazed a trail for administrators who wanted to become more connected.

Blogging has since become a reflective tool for Spike. After establishing his blog, *Insights Into Learning* (drspikecook .com), he quickly began to realize the benefits of sharing his personal insights as a principal, husband, father, and teacher. This platform also facilitated the development and communication of his shared vision through conveying the image of his ultimate educational setting. While using the tool to impart his vision and enhance communication practices with his teachers, he found they began to follow his lead. Before he knew it, he was beginning to see the changes he had set in motion.

Spike realized that to be a digital leader, he would need to commit to reading information on leadership daily and blog at least weekly to set the example for his peers and his teachers. He felt that the consistency of his commitment would not only lead to increased personal knowledge, but also build capacity among his teachers. He developed a plan to have his teachers become the most connected in the district. He felt that by arming the teachers with the necessary tools to integrate twenty-first-century technology, they would eventually become more effective teachers—and the students would benefit. A few had already begun to take steps to embrace the early stages of transformation.

Spike knew that in order to have sustainable change in his organization, he needed to empower a few risk takers. He did this by meeting both formally and informally with these key stakeholders. His main objective was to build resonance and to begin a two-way information-sharing protocol for improving their school. Fortunately for Spike, he had several teachers who were pursuing their master's degrees in educational technology. These teachers joined him and felt reinvigorated by their new principal's excitement with educational technology, seeing this as a way to integrate technology in more classrooms.

In order to expose the entire faculty to the changes in Spike's leadership, he scheduled a meeting to discuss his forays into social media. He felt compelled to share the news with the teachers because he knew that they would benefit from it. After this first meeting, the literacy coach and seven of his teachers signed up for Twitter or updated their existing accounts. Suddenly, numerous educators in his school were talking about social media and discussing whether or not they would take the plunge. Spike knew that in order to get beyond the staff's initial interest in social media, he needed a mechanism to build momentum.

Soon afterward, he began to slowly change his communication style with his teachers. Prior to his transformation, he would send out a weekly e-mail similar to a Monday Memo or Friday Focus (Whitaker, 2003). He wanted to get beyond the e-mail and create a place where teachers, students, and parents could meet in an interactive form of the Monday Memo. He created the RM Bacon Weekly School Blog as a weekly update of all the activities that were going on and a reflection on the accomplishments that the school made the week past. In this blog, there were videos, pictures, and relevant information carefully designed to increase learning and twenty-first-century skills as they told the story of the school.

It was during this time that he was approached by his literacy coach and another teacher who wanted to build a professional development program that would allow the staff to experience educational technology in terms of how it could benefit students. They created "Tech Fridays," designing them in the image of the "unconference" models of professional development they had seen popping up around the country. For the most part, these Tech Fridays have sustained the change needed to provide teachers with hands-on resources to better integrate technology into the classroom.

Spike began to see the transformation when the district held its annual Technology Showcase. His school had the most participation throughout the eleven schools in the district. Suddenly, there were community members who were asking about his school and suggesting that all schools embark on a similar technology revolution to that happening at Spike's school.

In addition to the Tech Fridays and the informal networking, Spike began to utilize his faculty meetings as opportunities to expose his teachers to technological tools that could assist them in the classroom. He encouraged teachers to bring their devices to the meetings and then showed them tools such as Poll Everywhere and Remind101. He presented these sites and modeled how the staff could easily stay connected with parents through mass text messaging.

Armed with his district-provided iPad, Spike saw the importance of using the iMovie application as a way for the school to create quick, professional-looking videos. At a staff meeting, after showing a video he had made, Spike offered the faculty the use of his iPad. A group of fifth-grade teachers took him up on the offer and created a video for the fifth-grade students. Soon afterward, teachers who taught other grade levels began to use the iPad or their own devices to create videos with their students. These videos showcased not only the effective use of technology, but also other programs and initiatives that increased their pride in their school.

To Spike, summer is not a time to slow down, but rather an opportunity to continue his pursuit of digital leadership. He maintained his social media and blogging schedule throughout the summer, and he realized that his teachers did as well. They were connecting with one another about their plans for the upcoming school year through Twitter, Edmodo, Facebook, and Pinterest. They shared ideas to improve not only how they used technology, but also student discipline, curriculum alignment, and time management. Upon their return from the summer break, there was an increase in activity among the staff in terms of social media and effective technology integration focused on enhancing learning (Cook, 2013).

Spike has never mandated technology integration. He has never asked a teacher to do something with which he or she was uncomfortable. Instead, he feels that modeling (Kouzes & Posner, 2007) is the effective leadership route to help his teachers grow. He rewards teachers who take risks and supports all teachers in what they need to be successful. He understands that each teacher develops connections in his or her own way, and exhibits patience with those who may never get beyond Web 1.0 tools.

His school has benefited from the sustained, focused change in technology and innovation, regularly making connections with other schools and educators through Skype, Twitter, Pinterest, Facebook, and blogging. He had a group of fourth-grade students last year connect with other fourth graders in Wisconsin, hosted several mystery Skype calls, and has had groups visit other schools to learn and collaborate. He has begun to bring in outside presenters to assist teachers with more advanced technology integration and support.

Since the Millville Public School District uses the McREL administrative walk-through program, Spike uses one of the features to track the data on his staff's use of technology. For instance, during the 2011–2012 school year, teachers at his school were observed using technology 29% of the observed time. Spike shared this information with the faculty at the conclusion of the year and vowed to help them raise the use of technology focused on learning goals for the upcoming school year. In the subsequent four months of observations, the staff increased their usage to 42% of the observed time. Student use of technology was observed to be 45% of the observed time in the 2012–2013 school year, up from 32% in the 2011–2012 school year. Utilizing the McREL administrative software has allowed Spike to chart the data on the school and provide observable reports that show how technology integration has increased under his leadership.

Spike credits Facebook with learning more about his teachers' personal lives. Since becoming friends on Facebook with his teachers, he can better understand his teachers' life changes, interests, and family. He feels that Facebook networking has also increased his staff's knowledge of one another, thereby aiding to the collaborative culture of the school. Teachers are able to communicate with one another beyond the constraints of the traditional school day and year.

As for Twitter, his teachers now find their own articles or information out there to help their classes and end up sharing this information with Spike. With more than 60% of his teachers on Twitter, he has seen ideas become reality. For instance, over the summer, teachers were searching for ways to improve their classroom management plans. Through Twitter, an article on Classdojo was circulated among the staff. Classdojo, an interactive classroom management application, provides teachers and students with opportunities to reward positive behaviors and track negative behaviors. Spike utilizes the data from the teachers to communicate with students and their parents. About 50% of the staff uses Classdojo, either through their interactive whiteboard, smartphone, or iPad.

Some of his teachers have started their own blogs in order better to reflect on their teaching and gain increased parental engagement. They have taken the practices that Spike modeled for the school and applied them at the classroom level. The teachers who have their own blogs are getting more parents involved and begging to "flip" their classrooms in order to enhance the learning process.

Spike has become a more effective principal and a more effective leader through his commitment to twenty-first-century learning. He has gained a global perspective on the successes and problems in education. He correlates his effectiveness with the systemic processes that he initiated to support his teachers. He feels that he has created an atmosphere that encourages teachers and students to take risks with new technology. Now that his school has embraced the transformation process, his vision is no longer singular in thinking but plural in practice.

THE SIX SECRETS OF CHANGE

Spike's journey provides a powerful lesson for all leaders: We must be the change that we wish to see in our schools (or in education, in general, for that matter). Leaders today typically choose one of two paths to follow: telling people what they want to hear or taking them where they need to be. Telling them what they want to hear will only help to strengthen the status quo and continue down a path of doing things the way they have been done forever. This path is also guided by that little voice in all of our heads that continually whispers, "If it isn't broke, why fix it?" The bottom line is that many of our schools are broken, because our techniques have not shifted in line with societal changes.

Any change process needs a starting point. The keys to sustainable change rely on identifying the problem(s), developing implementation plans to improve school culture, and anticipating future changes. Before moving ahead with change, process leaders should possess the appropriate knowledge to guide them during the process. Leading change expert Michael Fullan (2008), through his extensive work in this area, identified Six Secrets of Change (Figure 3.1).

Figure 3.1   The Six Secrets of Change

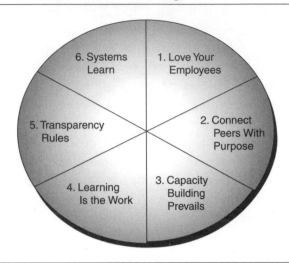

Source: Fullan (2008). Used with permission.

When reflecting on Spike Cook's journey, one can see how Fullan's change secrets were put into practice, learning to make sustainable changes in school culture. The end result was the creation of a learning environment at R. M. Bacon Elementary School that was more attuned with the active learners they were educating and a staff eager to embrace innovative practices. Putting the wheels of digital leadership in motion hinges on mastering the following six change secrets identified by Fullan (2008).

Fullan Change Secret 1: Love Your Employees

Explore the importance of building the school by focusing on the teachers and staff, students, and the community. The key is enabling staff to learn continuously while giving them a certain amount of autonomy to take risks and be innovative. Loving your employees is about helping them all find meaning, increased skill development, and personal satisfaction by making contributions that simultaneously fulfill their own goals and the goals of the organization (Fullan, 2008, p. 25). The best way to love your employees in order to initiate sustainable change is to trust and support them unconditionally.

Fullan Change Secret 2: Connect Peers With Purpose

Purposeful peer interaction within and beyond the school is crucial. Student learning and achievement increase substantially when teachers work in learning communities supported by school leaders who focus on improvement. It is also essential to develop relatable goals and associated outcomes with every change initiative. The *why* and the *how* need to be clearly articulated to the staff, and they need to be active participants in the change process. Purposeful peer interaction allows teachers to have a voice in the decision-making process and to craft how policies and mandates will be implemented (DuFour, DuFour, & Eaker, 2008).

Fullan Change Secret 3: Capacity Building Prevails

The most effective strategies involve helping teachers and principals develop the instructional and management of change skills necessary for school improvement. Capacity building concerns competencies, resources, and motivation. Individuals and groups are high in capacity if they possess and continue to develop these three components in concert (Fullan, 2008). At the core of the capacity-building model is distributed leadership along with social cohesion and trust (Hopkins & Jackson, 2003). The effectiveness of distributed leadership resides in the human potential available to be released within an organization, an emergent property of a group or network of individuals in which group members pool their expertise (Gronn, 2000). Leaders must continue to develop capacity in all stakeholders while always anticipating the next course of action. Studies on school change indicate that schools successful in sustaining school improvement build capacity for leadership within the organization (Harris & Lambert, 2003).

Fullan Change Secret 4: Learning Is the Work

Professional development (PD) in workshops, courses, and online environments is only one input to continuous learning and precision in teaching. Successful growth itself is accomplished when the culture of the school supports the day-to-day learning of teachers engaged in improving what they do in the classroom and school. Leaders must not only be creative in finding time for teachers to engage in PD during the day, but they also must consistently model lifelong learning themselves. Digital leadership dictates that learning is first and foremost.

Fullan Change Secret 5: Transparency Rules

Ongoing data, access to seeing effective practices, sharing innovation for others to learn from, and embracing digital tools are necessary for success. It becomes normal and desirable for teachers to observe and be observed in teaching facilitated by coaches and mentors. This is equally important when it comes to leaders sharing and seeing the work of their peers. Leaders, proud of the work being done in their schools, now have the means to continuously tell their story to key stakeholders. Sharing more information will increase engagement in the change process.

Fullan Change Secret 6: Systems Learn

Continuous learning depends on developing many leaders in the school in order to enhance continuity. It also depends on schools being confident in the face of complexity and open to new ideas. This holds true in a digital world. With the tools now available, leaders are no longer confined by space and time in their efforts to build capacity in and learn with others to improve professional practice. New ideas are being shared at a furious pace in online spaces, but change does not have to be a reinventing of the wheel. Instead, it can be that an idea that has been tested successfully elsewhere is adapted to meet the unique characteristics of one's own school or district.

OVERCOMING POTENTIAL ROADBLOCKS TO CHANGE

Fullan's Six Secrets of Change provide a great framework with which to begin the change process, but change can only be sustained if potential roadblocks are acknowledged throughout the process. Putting them on the table at the outset will help to create a vision and plan for implementation. If identified and addressed appropriately, roadblocks like those outlined below can be overcome.

1. **This is too hard.** News flash: CHANGE IS NOT EASY! Please keep this in mind as I continue this post. Change in the field of education is as elusive as the Loch Ness Monster. If it were easy, we would see countless examples of innovative programs, authentic learning experiences, successful integration of technology, and students yearning to arrive at school each day. The fact of the matter is that nothing in life comes easily, let alone transformational change in education. Educators must be willing to take risks, learn from mistakes, and put in the time.

2. **I don't have the time for this.** Ah, the old "time" excuse. This is probably the most common excuse given when educators and the thought or sight of change come together. We are in a profession with the opportunity to make a difference in the lives of children, leave a lasting impact, motivate them to achieve, instill a sense of lifelong learning, and prepare them for success once they leave our schools. If someone says they don't have time to work toward change that helps to achieve these goals,

then they should question why they are in the field of education. Dedicated educators make the time because it is their job! You ask any child who had a teacher that turned his or her life around, and he or she will tell you that the time spent was priceless!

3. **Lack of collaboration.** The field of education has been moving from a profession that hoarded ideas, lessons, and successful strategies to one that is openly willing to share this bounty with as many passionate educators as possible. Innovation and change are a collective process, and schools that understand this concept have personnel who routinely collaborate among one another and with those outside of their schools. "Together we are better" is the motto by which change agents abide.

4. **Directive approach.** Okay, I have been guilty of this when trying to get my staff to utilize Skype. Thankfully, I learned from this mistake and have found that change occurs through shared decision making, consensus, collaboration (see #3), and modeling. As a leader, I had better be able to effectively model what I want my teachers to implement if I have any hopes of seeing the idea succeed and be sustainable. In education, you can't just tell someone to do something because you were mesmerized by a piece of technology, read the latest book on innovative practices, or heard a great speaker discuss professional learning communities. You need to get each and every stakeholder involved in the process (see #3), properly model the strategy, and put the time forth to ensure successful implementation (see # 1 and 2).

5. **Hierarchy in schools.** The hierarchical structure in many schools is most often a deterrent to innovation and change. This results in a directive approach (see #4) being prevalent and no chance of collaboration being possible (see #3) because ideas have to go through many layers and red tape even to be considered. Schools that have moved away from a hierarchical structure support

learning cultures that are innovative. Educators need to be placed in environments where flexibility and freedom to take risks and try out new ideas and initiatives without fear of repercussion are actively fostered.

6. **No support.** As leaders, how can we expect teachers to be innovative and move toward change if we don't support them 100% of the time?

7. **Fear of change.** This is a given, so it had better be expected. If #1–5 above are addressed, this will help to alleviate fear. Passion for helping kids succeed will always work to one's advantage when trying to subdue the fear a group might experience in trying to initiate new ideas. Passion is what drives us! Use it to your advantage.

8. **The naysayers and antagonists.** Well, you should have known this was coming. Some people will never get on board with the change process for a variety of reasons, none of them good ones. Those who embrace change and experience success should be celebrated, honored, and commended. This is the best way to motivate others and inspire them to willingly become part of the process.

9. **Poor professional development.** How many times have we sat through training sessions that were boring, meaningless, and didn't provide any practical implementation ideas? Professional development has to be relevant to teachers, contain numerous choices, and be hands-on. More often than not, this can be done with teacher leaders present in all buildings. If money is going to be spent, make sure it is on vetted, well-respected presenters, where you will get your money's worth.

10. **Frivolous purchases.** Money does not equate to innovation and change. Just because you purchase the latest technology doesn't mean everyone will use it correctly or productively. Professional development (see #9) is key.

SUMMARY

Initiating and sustaining change does not have to be a cumbersome process fraught with insurmountable challenges. Fullan's (2008) Six Secrets to Change provide a framework from which leaders can work to initiate change. Sustaining change is accomplished not only by dealing with apparent roadblocks as they appear, but also by recognizing potential ones before they happen. Digital leadership is not only a change in mindset, but also a change in professional behavior that will pave the way to create a more relevant school through the seamless integration of twenty-first-century tools. It is not about changing who we are as leaders, but changing the way we do things that will transform school culture to better meet the needs of all stakeholders in the digital age.

4

Leading With Technology

"Leading in a culture of change means creating a culture (not just a structure) of change. It does not mean adopting innovations, one after another; it does mean producing the capacity to seek, critically assess, and selectively incorporate new ideas and practices—all the time, inside the organization as well as outside it."

—Fullan (2001, p. 44)

A SUPERINTENDENT'S JOURNEY

Lieutenant Colonel David Britten, retired following twenty-two years of military service, brought the importance of teamwork in planning and executing any mission with him to his second career as a public school administrator. He knows that effective teamwork requires that each member fully understand the vision, mission, and plan of execution from the standpoint of the role each member of the team plays in achieving success. There is no room for isolation. Failure to comprehend the role and expectations of each team member, from the leader down to the lowest-ranking soldier, increases the risk of failure.

Those lessons have informed his leadership style as an educational administrator these past seventeen years, and technology continues to expand his ability to "lead out loud," with a level of transparency that ensures all members of his team—administrators, teachers, students, parents, and the community—have the real-time information they need to contribute effectively to success. Social networking and blogging have given Britten the interactive tools that not only inform his decision making, but have also built a level of trust the Godfrey-Lee Public School District (Grand Rapids, Michigan) has never before experienced.

While evidence is not yet available to link real-time, interactive technology tools directly to increased academic achievement, Britten knows beyond a doubt that they have led to a change in climate and culture throughout his district that has raised the level of student learning significantly. In the nearly five years he has served as superintendent, bringing with him a broad vision of using technology tools in teaching, learning, and communicating, the community has witnessed its high school advance from one of the lowest achieving in the state to ranking in the top third of all public schools in Michigan. This has been brought about by a culture that no longer accepts the idea of low expectations for students in a poor, limited-English-speaking district, and its hybrid 1:1 and Bring Your Own Device (BYOD) technology vision has been at the core of this transformation.

Britten's motto is "Leading out loud," and he uses social networking and blogging to model both professional learning and transparent leadership for his administrative team. In recent years, with public education under attack by state leaders and legislators, he's led the local effort to advocate for equity in school funding and a broader concept of college and career readiness, unabashedly using Twitter, Facebook, and his personal Rebel 6 Ramblings blog site to point out the shortcomings in state and federal policies. Britten believes that not only have these tools become effective methods for communicating the concerns of the district regarding legislation and funding priorities, but also ensure that everyone throughout the district has real-time updates of information needed to join the effort. Using these tools appropriately and effectively models the important skills students can use as they develop their own advocacy roles.

Beyond the Godfrey-Lee District, Britten has used technology tools for his own professional learning and developing connections with educational leaders around the world. The use of Twitter in particular has led to several valuable partnerships-friendships that provide him with a convenient, real-time mechanism for bouncing off ideas and learning from others such as Pam Moran, superintendent of Albemarle County Schools in Virginia; Dave Doty, superintendent of Canyons Public Schools in Utah; and myself, principal of New Milford High in New Jersey. The professional life of an educational leader is often isolated and lonely, but technology has opened up a whole new avenue for developing learning and social relationships that can support a more successful career (Britten, 2013).

The future of educational leadership promises to become even more exciting as real-time communications through social networking and blogging combine with the expanding realm of analytics to provide administrators like Britten with more powerful, mission-focused tools. The right information focused on the needs of the moment and communicated in real time can only ensure that every member of the team contributes to student learning and organizational success.

DRIVING CHANGE

Recently, my school was recognized as the "School of the Month" for November/December by *eSchool News*. The resulting article described New Milford High School's many accomplishments pertaining to the use of educational technology to enhance the teaching and learning process. We are extremely proud of the culture that now exists, where technology is seen as one of many tools that are pivotal to student achievement and overall success. As technology's role in society continues to become more prevalent, it makes sense to integrate it effectively in schools so that our students are not shortchanged upon graduation.

New Milford High is a far cry from its former self. The many shifts, changes, and resulting transformation did not occur overnight, impulsively, or without calculated risks. As I look back on our journey and the path that was taken, I have been able to identify some key elements that have driven change. It was these changes that took an average, comprehensive high school and transformed it into the cutting-edge institution that many have come to know through social media over the past three years.

Three years ago, technology was viewed as an expensive frill that we would love to have but that was not worth the money when push came to shove. To me, being a technology leader meant making sure our computer labs were up to date and available for staff to use when needed. The notion of using social media was never a thought, since the perception was that it lacked any potential value for learning or education in general. As for cell phones, the only role they served was as a communication tool for students as they journeyed to and from school. Never under any circumstances would they have been used for learning during my early tenure as principal.

The above paragraph provides a brief, honest synopsis of where we were just a few years ago and the role I played in creating the exact opposite school culture described in the *eSchool News* piece. So what changed? How did New Milford become a technology-rich school where potential and promise are emphasized rather than problems, challenges, and excuses? How were we able to get everyone on board to initiate and sustain change? Here are some answers to these questions.

Connectedness Matters

It wasn't until I become connected that I truly understood the error of my ways and views. My social media journey has been well documented, but it was this journey that provided me with the knowledge, tools, and ideas needed to initiate change. Knowledge is everything, and it influences our decisions and opinions. For me, I lacked the fundamental knowledge of how technology could truly be integrated effectively. Once connected through social media, I was given the knowledge I desperately needed. For my school, connectedness was the original catalyst for change. It also enabled us to form numerous collaborative partnerships with an array of stakeholders who have assisted us along the way.

Vision

The seeds for change will only germinate if a coherent vision is established. It is important that all stakeholder groups contribute to a concrete, collective vision and work to create a plan for integration that clearly articulates why and how technology will be used to support education. Without the crucial *why* and *how,* any resulting plan will fail.

Value

One of the drawbacks to educational technology is the perceived lack of value it has in terms of student learning and achievement. With current reform efforts placing a greater emphasis on standardized test scores, the value of technology in the eyes of many has diminished or is nonexistent. The true value of technology rests on how it is used to support learning and create experiences that students find meaningful and relevant. This, in my opinion, is the key and should be included when establishing a vision. Technology has the power to engage students, unleash their creativity, and allow them to apply what they have learned to demonstrate conceptual mastery. If stakeholders understand and experience technology's value firsthand, change quickly follows.

Support

Support comes in many forms. Teachers need to have a certain amount of access to technology in order to experience the types of changes that have occurred at New Milford High. We made a commitment at the district level to install a wireless network four years ago and have consistently upgraded it over the years to its current 100mb/s capacity. This allows for the seamless and uninterrupted use of mobile devices by both teachers and students. We also made a commitment to transform a very old building (circa 1928) by outfitting rooms with the latest technology. This was a slow process that has occurred over the past three-and-a-half years. To put some perspective on this, not one traditional classroom had an interactive whiteboard (IWB) in it four years ago. Currently, we have twenty. In addition to providing access to technology, another essential support structure is removing the fear of failure and encouraging a risk-taking environment that fuels innovation. Driving change does not happen without this element. As a leader, it wasn't until I addressed my technology fears head on and then began to model technology's effective use that many of our initiatives began to flourish.

Professional Development

Without this element in place, change surely will not occur. Transforming a school culture based on significant shifts in pedagogy requires opportunities to learn how to effectively integrate technology. As there were not many quality professional development options in place when we started our journey, we made our own. This was accomplished by leveraging our teacher leaders and available resources. The majority of the knowledge, ideas, and strategies came from the formation of a Personal Learning Network (PLN). By harnessing the power of a PLN, I was able to impart what I learned to my staff. Trainings on various Web 2.0 tools were held after school. A year later, the Edscape Conference (edscapeconference.com) was formed to provide more relevant and meaningful growth opportunities. The most recent initiative involved the creation of a Professional Growth Period (PGP), a job-embedded growth model. This resulted in giving my staff the time and flexibility to learn how to integrate the tools that they were interested in, as well as to form their own PLNs.

Embracement

The final element that I found to be critical in driving change was empowering my staff to embrace technology as opposed to securing buy-in. To me there is a huge difference. Embracement is attained through empowerment and autonomy, as described above. Buy-in requires a salesman-like approach that might contain if-then rewards. We have no mandates to use technology at New Milford High School. Empowering teachers to shift their instructional practices and giving them the needed autonomy to take risks and work on effective integration techniques worked to intrinsically motivate them to change. This approach was found to be instrumental in our recent renaissance, minimizing resistance and resentment. Here are some guiding questions to begin the change process in one's digital leadership journey:

- How can educators and schools effectively use free social media tools such as Twitter and Facebook to communicate important information (e.g., student honors, staff accomplishments, meetings, emergency information) to stakeholders in real time?
- How can leaders take control of their public relations and produce a constant stream of positive news? If we don't share our story someone else will, and we then run the risk that it will not be positive.
- How do busy leaders go about establishing a brand presence once restricted to the business world when

schools and districts now have the tools at their finger-tips to do this in a cost-effective manner?

- How can leaders connect with experts and peers across the globe to grow professionally through knowledge acquisition, resource sharing, and engaged discussion, and to receive feedback?
- How can digital leaders create policies and environments that allow educators to use free social media tools to engage learners, unleash their creativity, and enhance learning?
- Is enough being done to teach students about digital responsibility/citizenship through the effective use of social media?
- How, or are, leaders tapping into countless opportunities that arise through conversations and transparency in online spaces?
- When will the profession of education catch up to society?

During my early years as New Milford High School principal (2007–2009), I had a vastly different perspective and philosophy as to what constituted a twenty-first-century learning environment. Back then, I felt that being a tech-savvy leader just consisted of purchasing the tools for my staff and letting them use them as they saw fit. I was also adamant that social media had no place in an educational setting. To put it bluntly, no educational organizations in the country would have even thought of approaching me to talk about the innovative use of technology at my school.

We have seen many shifts in terms of instruction, communication, and learning at New Milford High, resulting in a transformative culture that is more able to meet the needs of our students. So what changed? There wasn't one really big "Aha!" moment or school epiphany, but rather small changes on the surface that have resulted in some significant changes. The first small change was my philosophical enlightenment as to the educational value of Web 2.0 technologies, including social media. It was at this time that I saw the error of my ways and began to leverage the power of a PLN to effectively integrate an array of tools that I had never even heard of before. This small change evolved into my present philosophy on how schools can and should use social media. This short list includes

- Effectively communicating with stakeholders
- Establishing a consistent public relations platform
- Developing a brand presence that promises value
- Authentically engaging students in the learning process
- Providing cost-effective professional development that is meaningful
- Discovering opportunity for my school
- Rethinking how the learning environment was structured

The second small change was educating my staff on the value of Web 2.0 technologies in the classroom and beyond. Instead of mandating that every teacher integrate technology, I chose to empower my staff to create a stimulating learning environment. Little things such as support, encouragement, flexibility, and modeling have gone a long way to provide my staff with the confidence to take risks with technology and create meaningful learning activities that foster creativity, problem solving, and participation by all students. This is now a collaborative effort, and more and more teachers are beginning to embrace a vision that pairs sound pedagogical techniques with technology.

The third small change was realizing that students had to be instrumental in any effort to transform the culture of our school. We had to give up a certain amount of control in order to successfully implement a BYOD program where students are granted access to the school's wireless network during the day using their computing devices. We also had to trust that they would use their mobile learning devices (i.e., cell phones) responsibly as a tool for learning in certain classes using free programs such as Poll Everywhere.

The fourth and final small change was becoming a more transparent administrator and sharing the innovative practices taking place within the walls of my school. With Twitter, I have been able to give my stakeholders a glimpse into my role as an educational leader. Facebook has been an incredible tool to share real-time information, student achievements, and staff innovations. Both of these tools combined have given my stakeholders and the greater educational community a bird's-eye view into my school and the great things happening here.

These small changes, combined with many others, are beginning to have a huge impact on the teaching, learning, and community culture of my school. They are also the basis for the Pillars of Digital Leadership. Even though I have highlighted changes specific to technology, there have also been those focused on curriculum and programming. Politicians and self-proclaimed reformers routinely throw around the word *change*, and think that a one-size-fits-all approach is what's needed to increase student achievement and innovation. Each school is an autonomous body with distinct dynamics that make it unique. It's the small changes over time that will eventually leave a lasting impact. Schools and educators need to be empowered to make these changes as they see fit. These are the keys to learning with technology.

The Pillars of Digital Leadership

It is incumbent upon leaders to address the above questions, because they hold the key to introducing practical change to leadership and school culture. The Pillars of Digital Leadership represent a basis from which new ideas and practices evolve in order to improve schools and professional practices. Embedded within each pillar are new skills and behaviors that develop either to complement traditional models and methods of effective leadership or create entirely new pathways of doing things. Each provides a context for leaders to lead in different ways that are aligned with societal shifts that place an increased demand on technological fluency and integration. They also connect to or fit in with existing national technology standards and frameworks for school improvement in the twenty-first century. The effective integration of readily available technology—especially social media—serves as the main foundation of each pillar. This dynamic resource, available for free to leaders, can be leveraged as a multidimensional leadership tool to spark involvement, creativity, and discussions that truly matter. Once the conversations begin, the seeds of change will quickly be planted. The Seven Pillars of Digital Leadership include

1. Communication

2. Public relations

3. Branding

4. Professional growth and development

5. Student engagement and learning

6. Opportunity

7. Learning environment and spaces

ISTE NETS•A

The Pillars of Digital Leadership are aligned to the International Society for Technology in Education's (ISTE) National Educational Technology Standards for Administrators (NETS•A) (ISTE, 2009). These represent the standards for evaluating the skills and knowledge school leaders need to support digital-age learning, implement technology, and transform the educational landscape. Transforming schools into digital-age places of learning requires leadership from people who can accept new challenges and embrace new opportunities, which is at the heart of digital leadership. Now more than ever, the success of technology integration depends on leaders who can implement systemic reform in schools. A list and description of all the NETS•A can be found in Appendix A. Leaders can utilize the NETS•A as guidelines as they work to implement change through the Pillars of Digital Leadership. Together, these will pave the way for transformational change.

Breaking Ranks Framework

The National Association of Secondary School Principals (NASSP) created a landmark framework fifteen years ago to assist leaders in making schools more student centered by personalizing programs and support systems to meet the intellectual challenges of each student. The *Breaking Ranks* Framework (NASSP, 2011) is a powerful tool for leaders, as it does not prescribe a specific model that a school must follow, but rather builds upon the individual school's data and existing culture to assess strengths and identify needs so that a customized plan for school success can be developed. The Pillars of Digital Leadership are a natural fit for the *Breaking Ranks* Framework, since each focuses on school improvement through the lens of practicing leaders.

The *Breaking Ranks* Framework has leaders focus on and address three core areas: collaborative leadership (CL); personalizing your school environment (PER); and curriculum, instruction, and assessment to improve student performance (CIA). By addressing each of these three overlapping areas, leaders can implement change to improve student performance and overall school culture. Digital leadership integrates technology and essential skill sets as the catalysts for change detailed in the *Breaking Ranks* Framework. Figure 4.1 illustrates the entire framework.

At the foundation of the interconnected *Breaking Ranks* Framework lie nine cornerstones and twenty-nine interconnected recommendations within the three core areas (collaborative leadership, personalizing your school environment, curriculum/instruction/assessment) that guide implementation of improvement initiatives. These are the foundational concepts upon which the *Breaking Ranks* Framework is built.

Figure 4.1   NASSP *Breaking Ranks* **Framework**

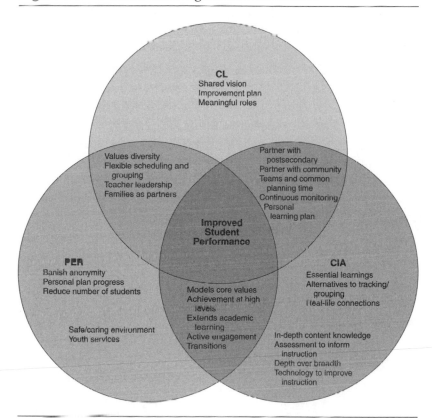

CL
Shared vision
Improvement plan
Meaningful roles

Values diversity
Flexible scheduling and
grouping
Teacher leadership
Families as partners

Partner with
postsecondary
Partner with community
Teams and common
planning time
Continuous monitoring
Personal
learning plan

Improved
Student
Performance

PER
Banish anonymity
Personal plan progress
Reduce number of students

CIA
Essential learnings
Alternatives to tracking/
grouping
Real-life connections

Models core values
Achievement at high
levels
Extends academic
learning
Active engagement
Transitions

Safe/caring environment
Youth services

In-depth content knowledge
Assessment to inform
instruction
Depth over breadth
Technology to improve
instruction

Source: NASSP (2011). Used with permission.

Note. CL refers to collaborative leadership; PER refers to personalizing your school environment; CIA refers to curriculum, instruction, and assessment to improve student performance.

These include leadership, professional development, culture, organization, curriculum, instruction, assessment, relationships, and equity.

It is incumbent upon leaders to determine a plan of action when integrating the Pillars of Digital Leadership as catalysts for transformational change. Leading with technology is no different than any other change process. A systematic approach that emphasizes each pillar will not only implement and sustain change at the school level but at the personal professional level as well. The *Breaking Ranks* Framework emphasizes six stages of systematic school improvement (Figure 4.2) that will greatly assist school leaders as they integrate the Pillars of Digital Leadership. The pillars provide points of reference to improve leadership behaviors, practices, and strategies with the assistance of technology. They will also lay the foundation for rethinking how learning spaces and time are structured in order to provide more personalized experiences for all stakeholders by institutionalized autonomy, mastery, and purpose.

Figure 4.2   Six Stages of Systematic School Improvement

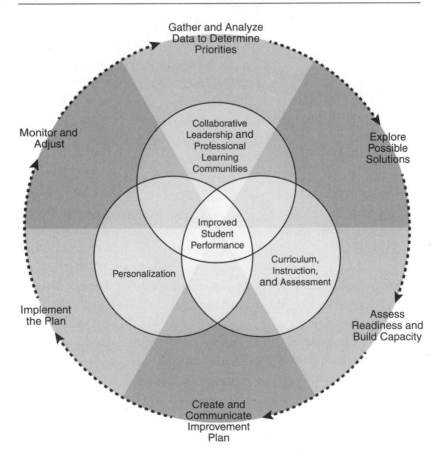

SUMMARY

As we move further into the digital age, it is imperative that school leaders develop a vision for the role that technology will play and establish a strategic plan for implementation across a broad spectrum. Moving from vision to action in this area can be accomplished by emulating the behaviors, techniques, and strategies utilized by highly effective technology leaders. Change in this regard requires establishing a clear vision, an inherent sense of value, embracement as opposed to buy-in, relevant professional development, and support. The Pillars of Digital Leadership provide the foundational elements to begin the process of transformational change using technological resources that perfectly align with national standards for technology leadership and frameworks for school improvement (Table 4.1).

Table 4.1   Standards and Framework for Digital Leadership

Digital Leadership Pillar	ISTE NETS•A	Breaking Ranks Framework
Communication	1, 3, and 5	CL[a]
Public Relations	1, 2, and 5	CL, PER[b]
Branding	2 and 4	CL
Professional Growth and Development	3	CL, CIA[c], PER
Student Engagement and Learning	1, 2, 3, 4, and 5	CL, CIA, PER
Learning Spaces and Environment	1, 2, and 4	CL, CIA, PER
Opportunity	1 and 4	PER

a. CL refers to collaborative leadership.

b. PER refers to personalizing your school environment.

c. CIA refers to curriculum, instruction, and assessment to improve student performance.

5

Communication

It's Tuesday night at 7:00 PM, and the monthly Home and School meeting is about to begin in the library at Knapp Elementary School in suburban Philadelphia, where Joe Mazza is the principal. The Home and School president begins by greeting the fourteen parents in attendance and then looks up at the big projector screen to welcome the forty-four parents logged in from home who are also participating via a live video feed. Parents "virtually" sign in and acknowledge their name, their child's grade, and provide a simple greeting.

The Home and School president begins the meeting by asking the principal to deliver a monthly report, which includes updates, new ideas, and other important announcements to engage families who are both in the room and tuning in from home via live video feed. The meeting continues over the next sixty minutes with conversations happening both physically and virtually. Parents without cars, without a babysitter, and without good mobility for whatever reason can participate virtually without the need to physically be in the room where the meeting takes place. The school meets the parents "where they are."

Just as teachers differentiate for a variety of learning styles in the classroom, it is important for schools to differentiate their communication efforts if we want true home/school partnerships. For school leaders, communication and community relations have been identified as one of the nine most important skills to master (Hoyle, English, & Steffy, 1998). It is difficult for any school leader to be successful if he or she cannot communicate effectively (Arnold, Perry, Watson, Minatra, & Schwartz, 2006). Joe Mazza has taken the lead in this area, and his school is benefitting from his efforts. Like our students, today's parents are also evolving in the tools they use each day as moms and dads. Technology—and social media specifically—has arrived. It is our job to keep current with the astronomical increase in technology use by our stakeholders.

When school leaders hear the words *Twitter* and *Facebook*, they cringe. Immediately, visions of excessive socialization, time wasted, and meaningless conversations in the form of updates come to mind. This is true, in many cases, when these tools are used for personal use. However, there are many ways in which schools and leaders can harness the power of these free resources to improve communications and ultimately improve their overall effectiveness and efficiency. Societal shifts have made traditional forms of communication such as snail mail, newsletters, website updates, and even e-mail irrelevant as many stakeholders no longer rely on or value these communication mediums. Digital leadership demands that we reach our stakeholders through the use of tools and social spaces that they frequent, as they have become accustomed to and dependent upon 24/7 access to information. It calls for a hybrid construct of communication techniques that blends the traditional methods mentioned above with the systematic use of social media tools to create a dynamic, two-way system that will increase engagement with all stakeholders.

THE TIME IS NOW

Social media provide many free tools that leaders can incorporate into their communications plan. They include Twitter,

Facebook, and blogs. Twitter has been rising in popularity across the globe. According to Twitter's website, 3.7 million Super Bowl–related tweets were sent on Super Bowl Sunday in 2012. With *460,000 new sign-ups happening each day*, Twitter is the fastest growing social media tool in the world. Facebook is still the social media of choice, but Twitter is gaining ground quickly. YouTube, LinkedIn, blogs, and wikis are also very popular social media being used today for personal and professional reasons. Something that gave Joe pause: The most popular age group of today's Twitter users is eighteen to thirty-five, the age of most parents with whom he currently works and will be working to build home/school partnerships at his elementary school (Pew Internet and American Life, 2011). Joe's experience has taught him that the easiest way to showcase Twitter for families is linking your school Twitter and Facebook pages so that each tweet sent from the school is automatically embedded onto the school's Facebook wall. Using social media tools that complement one another is extremely important, but to get to this point, it is important to understand the major social media tools available to school leaders and how they can be used to enhance communications.

Twitter

Twitter is a microblogging platform that allows users to send free messages called tweets in 140 characters or less. Tweets can be text, images, or even videos, making it a dynamic communications tool. The brevity and succinctness of tweets allow leaders to communicate real-time information that is not only impactful, but also saves precious time. Character limits and the ability of people to receive tweets as SMS text messages make this a powerful communications tool. Instead of spending money on expensive information delivery systems, digital leaders can use Twitter for free. One of the benefits of using Twitter is that you can communicate information whenever and wherever you want, making it extremely convenient.

Parents today are extremely busy, and it is often difficult to keep track of all of their children's events. Twitter provides a great medium for leaders to send out routine reminders of school functions such as concerts, art shows, athletic games, scholastic competitions, and Back-to-School Night. This not only keeps all stakeholders in the know, but also provides access to this information through a variety of mobile devices where traditional means of communication fall short.

There are a great many meetings that occur at schools, and they involve a variety of stakeholder groups. Leaders can use Twitter to send out meeting reminders (Parent-Teacher Organization/Association, Athletic Boosters, etc.); notify attendees of a room and/or time change; distribute agendas beforehand; and make the minutes of the meetings available to all, even if they were unable to attend the meeting. Of course, all of this information can be posted on a website, but chances are stakeholders are not frequenting these as much as they did in the past. The key again is to use social media tools not only to get the information quickly and easily to our stakeholders, but also to redirect them to other sources of information that provide more depth.

The second schools close due to weather or other issues, stakeholders want to know. Digital leadership calls for leaders to anticipate where current notification systems might fail and have backup plans or strategies in place. During Superstorm Sandy in the fall of 2012, New Milford High School and the town of New Milford were without power for days. This resulted in many parents and staff members not receiving the message sent out through the automated call system each night. Twitter and Facebook became invaluable communications tools in the storm's aftermath, as school-closing information was still pushed out and accessible through mobile devices.

Athletics are the hub of many schools, and it is near impossible to attend each and every event due to the number of teams and completion levels. With Twitter, school leaders can keep the avid sports fan in the community abreast of this information either through a school account or a separate one for the Athletic Department. New Milford High School did just this, because sports are a vital component of the school culture (twitter.com/NMHS_Athletics).

The success of our students should be celebrated at every opportunity. Twitter makes it easy for school leaders to capture, curate, and share student achievements and successes as they happen in a way that can be accessed by stakeholders no matter where they are. Tweets that celebrate and commend the work done by students are possibly the most influential type of communication today. These messages can be descriptions, pictures, or even videos that capture the moment. Think about the impact of communicating pictures from the art show, video from the winter concert, or updates on who is attending a college fair in your building.

Teachers are the backbones of our schools and, unfortunately, their innovative work is not shared as much as it should be. Twitter allows school leaders to create more of a transparent culture by tweeting out lessons, ideas, and innovative learning activities that are observed during classroom walk-throughs, formal observations, or just a daily stroll through the building.

In this day and age, a much greater emphasis has been placed on school security and communicating information to parents during times of crisis. School leaders must always be on the cutting edge and anticipate how they might dispense precious information if traditional means (radios, e-mail, P.A. system, landline phones, etc.) are unavailable or inoperable. Twitter on a mobile device solves this potential problem and can be used to keep all stakeholders informed during and after emergencies.

Effective communication is not just about making the news, but making sure that all stakeholders hear it. Whether in the form of a school newsletter or articles that appear in mainstream media outlets, Twitter can be used to send links to more detailed information about the school, recently adopted policies, scholarship opportunities, and construction projects. Social media have made it easier than ever for leaders to collect and curate resources for parents, teachers, and students.

Integrating the use of Twitter to communicate to stakeholders the available Internet resources that can extend learning beyond the school day builds support and appreciation for the work being done by the school.

At New Milford High School, I have created an official Twitter account (twitter.com/NewMilfordHS) to send out the above information. I developed a simple instruction sheet and disseminate it annually to all of my parents, because many people still don't really know what Twitter is or how it can be used for professional communications. It explains to parents how to sign up, activate updates on their cell phones, and the types of information that will be sent out. To get started with using Twitter as a school and professional communications tool, follow these simple steps:

1. Create a free account at twitter.com. For set-up tips and assistance, visit support.twitter.com.

2. Develop a username that reflects the use of this tool for school communications.

3. When establishing your account, make sure to include a biographical sketch, the link to the school or professional website, and an avatar (i.e., a picture of you or the school).

4. Add a background that showcases school pride, such as pictures of the building, your mascot, or your school colors.

5. Notify key stakeholders of the Twitter account and how it will be used for communications (Appendix B).

Facebook

As I learned from my students, many more people use the social media tool Facebook than use Twitter. Everyone seems to be on Facebook these days, including students, parents, grandparents, community members, and local businesses. At their advice, I created a Facebook page for New Milford High

School. This communications tool has now become the hub for everything we do at our school. It has become a conduit for school pride and connecting to alumni as a two-way communications medium. Schools and leaders that have introduced Facebook as a communications tool understand that stakeholders are no longer visiting static, boring websites that rely on one-way communication efforts. Digital leadership is driven by the desire to meet our stakeholders where they are, even if it is not comfortable at first. It is also about anticipating the risks of having an open Facebook page for two-way communication efforts and knowing how to deal with issues as they arise.

All stakeholder groups routinely comment on and like informational updates that are communicated using this social media tool. The same information sent out using Twitter is also placed on our New Milford High School Facebook page. The ultimate power of Facebook as a communications tool lies in its ability to foster community engagement through two-way communication. It is important for leaders in a digital world to understand the value and merit of allowing this engagement and interactivity. If a school Facebook page is just used as a tool to communicate information while not allowing comments and likes, then it is no different than a school website.

Getting started with Facebook as a communications tool is relatively easy, but you do need to have a personal account in order to create a Fan Page for your school or institution. Even though a personal account is needed, no one can access any of your information from any Fan Page that is created. To begin the process of creating a Facebook page for your school, visit www.facebook.com/pages/create.php. Once there, follow these simple steps:

1. Select Company, Organization, or Institution.

2. On the drop-down menu, select Education, add your school's name, and agree to Facebook's Terms of Service.

3. Add a profile picture of your school or mascot.

4. Completely fill out the About section by including a description of your school, website, mission statement, operating hours, map of location, and any other important links (e.g., Twitter feeds, athletic calendar, etc.).

5. Create a unique Facebook Web address.

6. Once the page is created, click "edit page" on the admin panel to manage the permissions for the page. It is important to select settings that support two-way communication.

With a new Facebook page as part of a communications plan, leaders can begin to further engage stakeholders. In addition to status updates, leaders can communicate information through the uploading of pictures and videos. Events can easily be created that will keep all stakeholders in the know. There is even the ability to create polling questions to further engage stakeholders that visit the site. Measuring engagement can be determined by the number of "likes" and "impressions" on individual status updates on the page wall. "Impressions" refer to how many times a specific post was displayed within news feeds. Leaders can easily see the impact of communicating through a Facebook page with integrated analytic features on the admin page. By clicking on the "insights" graph, a much more detailed graph appears providing analytic data on each day and post.

Using Facebook and Twitter together allows leaders to deliver positive information into the hands of stakeholders. Where leaders once relied on the media, press releases, and websites, they now have the ability to get out links to media articles and website updates as well as pictures and video that highlight school programs. By doing so, they ultimately enhance public relations (Chapter 6) and create a brand presence (Chapter 7) for their building, one that conveys a message of success, organization, innovation, and achievement. Table 5.1 lists K–12 schools that use both Twitter and Facebook as part of their communications plan.

Table 5.1   Schools Using Social Media for Communications

School	Twitter	Facebook
New Milford High School, New Milford, NJ	twitter.com/ NewMilfordHS	www.facebook.com/ NewMilfordHS
Waldwick High School, Waldwick, NJ	twitter.com/ WaldwickWHS	on.fb.me/WyS5rn
Arapahoe High School, Centennial, CO	twitter.com/ ahswarriors	www.facebook.com/ ahswarriors
Coppell High School, Coppell, TX	twitter.com/ CoppellHigh	on.fb.me/YeJsQ8
Black River Middle School, Chester, NJ	twitter.com/ BlackRiverMS	on.fb.me/14M8ADP
Harry H. Herndon Intermediate School, Royse City, TX	twitter.com/ herndonheros	on.fb.me/12ij8aX
Utica Junior High School, Utica, OH	twitter.com/ UticaJrHigh	on.fb.me/VmSz4u
Knapp Elementary School, Lansdale, PA	twitter.com/ knappelementary	www.facebook.com/ KnappElementary
Hermosa Schools, Hermosa, SD	twitter.com/ hermosaschools	www.facebook.com/ HermosaSchools
Hattiesburg School District, Hattiesburg, MS	twitter.com/ HPSD	www.facebook.com/ HattiesburgPSD

Principal Trailblazers

If you're part of a growing Personal Learning Network (PLN) on Twitter, you have instant access to cutting-edge communication strategies by many of today's most highly regarded leaders. Schools are beginning to respond to the increasing digital parent audience. However, only a small population is truly providing social media tools to connect families for reasons such as policy restrictions, fear, lack of trust, lack of supporting research, and lack of resources. Aside from my *New Milford High School* Facebook and Twitter accounts, some inspiring school examples to check out are Chris Lehmann's Science Leadership Academy High School (Facebook and Twitter) and Lyn Hilt's Brecknock Elementary (blog). Joe recommends hosting ongoing trainings for staff, administration, and parents throughout the school year to showcase the menu of communication offerings your school provides. Don't assume that all of your stakeholders already know how to use the tools you are using.

A MULTIFACETED APPROACH TO ENGAGING STAKEHOLDERS

Educators must be experts in effective communication techniques, especially when it comes to parents and other key stakeholders. As the times and tools have changed, we now have a variety of means to disseminate information in a more efficient and cost-effective fashion. There are four key principles that lay a foundation for communicating effectively with parents: transparency, honesty, accessibility, and flexibility. As you will see, these four principles can be applied to the following strategies that are listed below.

1. Make your professional e-mail and Twitter accounts available. This way, parents can contact you at their convenience. If you have not created such an account for your school, I highly recommend that you do so. During the beginning of each school year, I send home a letter to all parents that provides detailed information on what Twitter is, how to create an account, and configuring the settings to receive SMS text messages. This versatility, allowing parents to receive updates on their own terms, makes Twitter unlike any traditional communication tool that I've ever used as a principal. As far as transparency goes, there might not be an application more effective than Twitter. In response to parent feedback,

I created an "official" school account (@NewMilfordHS). The New Milford High School Twitter page includes a link to the school's main website as well as our school's colors, mascot, and logo. This makes our page stand out to viewers and establishes a brand presence. Information tweeted out from this account in real time includes sports scores, special schedules, school news, student achievements, staff accomplishments, campus weather, and emergency information.

2. Create your own website and include contact information, your availability to meet with or speak to parents, extra help hours, student assignments, press, etc. This is also a great way to convey to parents your philosophy on education, professional accomplishments, and vision for helping students succeed. My website can be viewed at cricsheninger.com.

3. Hold training workshops for parents. Many of them use social media tools on a personal level, but hands-on trainings provide a detailed look at both the *why* and the *how* they will be used to communicate better with stakeholders.

4. Call home on both positive and negative issues. Combining this traditional method of communication with that of social media will continue to build and maintain strong relationships. Leaders must never forget how powerful this type of communication is even in the digital age.

5. Share as many student and teacher accomplishments and success stories as possible. Parents want and need to hear the great things happening in our buildings and classrooms. Consider creating a monthly report or blog post that captures these moments. I have created the *Principal's Report* at New Milford High School that is communicated to our parents using our school website as well as Twitter and Facebook accounts. This can be viewed at www.newmilfordschools .org/NMHS/school_report.html.

6. Set up a separate phone number for parents using Google Voice. Google Voice is a free, Web-based phone service that leaders can use to set up a phone number for parents and

other stakeholders to call and leave messages. This number is totally separate from personal and/or school cell numbers and never actually "rings." Once a phone message is received, an e-mail containing a text transcript will be sent for the leader to follow-up on.

7. Make resources readily available for parents using a social bookmarking service such as Delicious or Diigo. Once these are curated, they become categorized resources with a description that can be communicated to parents using Twitter, Facebook, or e-mail. Leaders can even create separate resources for students and staff.

8. ALWAYS return parent phone calls and e-mails in a timely fashion! It is also extremely important to respond to tweets and Facebook comments to foster two-way communications while increasing stakeholder engagement.

9. Invite parents into your classrooms and schools. If parents cannot physically attend, leaders can now set up live video streams over the Internet using free tools such as Ustream and Google + Hangouts on Air.

10. Develop a school Facebook page to advertise events and provide up-to-date school information. As mentioned previously in this chapter, the New Milford High School Facebook page has now become our informational hub on which parents have come to rely.

11. Institute a positive referral policy and make parents aware when their child is recognized. This can be done traditionally with a phone call or e-mail, but can also be done publicly using social media tools such as Twitter or Facebook.

12. Start a blog, let parents know about it, and encourage them to comment on your posts. Blogs are fantastic communication tools where parents can glimpse your educational life and become more familiar with the culture of your school.

13. Look for other means to reach stakeholders. In my quest to create a paperless environment at New Milford High,

I discovered ZippSlip (www.zippslip.com). ZippSlip enables schools and parents to fully process paper forms online from any smartphone, tablet, or computer. All results are tracked and displayed by their cloud-based app that is 100% Health Insurance Portability and Accountability Act (HIPAA) and Family Educational Rights and Privacy Act (FERPA) compliant ensuring privacy. There's no training, and virtually no IT support is required. Leaders can leverage this two-way, fully secure channel for media-rich interactions with parents and the community. This free solution not only allows my parents to sign and submit all school forms electronically, but it also provides me with a portal to send e-mail and video messages to them.

If we're going to succeed as a school, we've got to get several different stakeholder groups—parents, students, community leaders, and businesses—to embrace a set of core beliefs. That means that digital leaders need to constantly try to craft messages that have resonance and to deliver those messages in ways that are likely to be heard. In many ways, communication is the most important thing I do every day.

Adding the "e" to FACE

Family and Community Engagement (FACE) has been well researched over multiple decades. Researchers like Dr. Joyce Epstein, Dr. Anne Henderson, and Dr. Karen Mapp have published a great deal on the importance of meeting parents where they are in terms of building home/school partnerships. Joe coined the term "eFACE," or electronic Family and Community Engagement. It uses technology tools to bridge home and school while creating and maintaining partnerships. According to Epstein (2011), true home/school partnerships call for communication to include plenty of two-way options, not just one-way sharing. The use of technology to support a comprehensive eFACE plan opens new doors by providing access to conversations already happening in virtual spaces such as Facebook, Twitter, YouTube, Google+, blogs, and wikis.

Joe insists that technology cannot be the magic bullet for home/school partnerships, but it can certainly complement the overall efforts. In an increasingly digital age, it is even more important to take the extra time necessary to maintain face-to-face communication with eye contact, respect, tone, and empathy as the ideal relationship builder whenever possible. Face-to-face, two-way communication should continue to be at the root of our communications efforts. Growing and fine-tuning these efforts along the way is vital. The feedback may or may not come while using technology; however, not offering these tools as a means of two-way communication limits those parents who *are* already comfortable with these tools. Much like we do in the classroom with students, parents need us to differentiate for their needs. Leaders should read *Beyond the Bakesale* (Davies, Henderson, Johnson, & Mapp, 2008), with particular attention to the four core beliefs of partnership with schools. Whichever communications (FACE and/or eFACE) you choose, the core beliefs you have in place should not change, and face-to-face communications should remain the foundation of your efforts.

eFACE—Electronic Family and Community Engagement Offerings

It is important to note that technology cannot replace face-to-face communications and the eye contact, tone, empathy, and mutual respect that speaking with someone face to face provides us as humans. Tools like Skype and Facetime now make opportunities for these discussions when physical meetings are not possible; however, Joe has found that while technology can complement our FACE efforts, it cannot replace them.

Through two-minute technology surveys, he found that 93% of his families were either on cell phones or computers with Internet access each day. With this data in mind, he crafted a menu of options for two-way communications. For those who did not have a computer and did not understand English, he sent home a translated hard copy of what was communicated, as it is imperative to understand and commit to equal access for all families.

The Evolution of eFACE

Knapp Elementary School began its eFACE efforts with a mass Google account set up to broadcast e-mails out to parents. After six years, it had over 500 e-mails included on this list. It has used this tool to link parents to various resources without sending large files, etc. While this is a nice first step to identify electronic addresses, it only serves as a one-way offering, and it doesn't provide much opportunity for two-way, back-and-forth communications.

Fast-forward the tape. It is now using technology as a means to solicit information directly from its families, which is the best way to communicate with them. Joe has built a solid partnership with the Home and School president, and they share many of the tools used to engage families, including a Family Engagement Wiki (knapp wiki.wikispaces.com). On that wiki (which means *quick* in Hawaiian), parents and teachers have added and archived resources and events for families. Instead of sending out large PDFs or Word documents and flyers, information is housed in the wiki, and parents are sent a link to the content.

Knapp Elementary chose to use a wiki because it was quick and easy to update content while serving as a two-way tool much like a blog. In staff members' busy roles, it had become increasingly important to spend more time with the students and staff and less struggling with the formatting of a website. Feedback from their families suggested that the wiki option provided a user-friendly interface with a great deal of information for new and veteran families to digest throughout the school year.

One of Knapp's family engagement goals has been to find ways to get more parents involved in the leadership of its Home and School Association. During its monthly meetings, only fifteen to twenty parents were coming out to participate in the discussion. At one particular Home and School meeting, a dialogue was held around how they needed to double their attendance at these meetings, draw from a greater cross-section of their school's population, respect parents' limited vehicle access, and understand the need for babysitting services—all this with no funds laying around to pay for whatever it was that would make this happen.

The following month they tried "Home & School 2.0," and broadcasted a LIVE audio and video feed of the meeting. Through this effort, they grew their monthly participation to over fifty participants, as referenced earlier. There are now student clubs presenting at the heart of each of these broadcasted meetings, which keeps the focus on students. Knapp Elementary School has a high population of working moms and dads, and many of them work two or more jobs. The feedback provided to Joe was that this new way of communicating was a better option for the busy parent in that they could now tune in from either home or work for free. One of the best parts of these meetings has been that several teachers also tune in and share during the meeting from the comfort of their own homes. Knapp Elementary School's full menu of family engagement offerings includes

- Twitter (@KnappElementary)—Daily classroom messages are tweeted out by Knapp Elementary staff and parents highlighting the learning that is taking place
- Facebook—Facilitated by the Home and School Association at www.facebook.com/knappelementary
- The Family Engagement Wiki (knappwiki.wikispaces .com)
- The Knapp Elementary Family Engagement App (free download Apple/Android)
- An eBully Reporting System, eBucket Filler, eVolunteer (all on app and wiki)
- Home & School 2.0—Monthly meetings broadcast from school and local community gathering places to encourage maximum participation from stakeholders

- Zippslip (www.zipplslip.com)—Private electronic mail interface, paperless forms, two-way feedback
- Google Textline—Texting options that come in and out of Joe's iPad
- Remind101 (www.remind101.com)—Text alert system for emergency cancellations
- Poll Everywhere (www.polleverywhere.com)—Real-time polls for meeting feedback
- Todays Meet (www.todaysmeet.com)—A backchannel tool that works much like Twitter without the need to log in
- KnappModo—Edmodo (www.edmodo.com) set-up for students in Grades 4–6 with parent access
- Google Picasa Photo Account for Knapp Elementary
- Google Translate—Located on each wiki page for parents who do not speak English fluently
- Language Line—A conference call interpreting service offered for every family
- KnappTV—YouTube channel for student broadcasts
- Audioboo—Knapp audio channel for quick school announcements
- Kidblog.org—Blogs through which students can share life at Knapp Elementary

SUMMARY

According to Bouffard (2008), the Internet represents a promising but largely untapped opportunity for promoting family–school communication. If we are serious about keeping children and public education in focus, schools can no longer afford to turn a blind eye to social media tools in their overall communication efforts and, specifically, in meeting the needs of all families. Educators can take advantage of a multitude of ideas and resources, using the very social media tools some are using to communicate with families (e.g., Twitter). If it were not for Twitter, Joe would not have been exposed to the numerous free technology tools mentioned earlier in this chapter with which he broadcasts monthly Home and School meetings for families, upgrading the two-way communications offered at Knapp Elementary School. With many leaders being forced to "do more with less," utilizing free tools to enhance communications has never been more vital. Digital leadership calls for getting information out to stakeholders through a variety of media, anticipating the tools to which they might have access, and fostering a culture that supports and promotes two-way communication.

6

Public Relations

"Again and again in history some special people in the crowd wake up. They have no ground in the crowd, and they emerge according to much broader laws. They carry strange customs with them, and demand room for bold actions. The future speaks ruthlessly through them. They save the world."

—Rainer Maria Rilke (1899)

Having served the Van Meter Community School District as secondary principal and superintendent and now as superintendent of schools for the Howard-Winneshiek Community School District in Iowa, John Carver understands the importance of creating a brand. By his utilizing social media, a voice is created, stakeholders are engaged, thinking is shared, and consensus can be built for facilitating change.

John feels that we are at a "printing press moment" in the history of humanity. The invention of the printing press amplified and shared thinking, eventually turning every system of its day upside down. The printed word empowered all who could read to explore and share knowledge and experiences. The Bible was made available to the masses, the Catholic Church fractured, governments were toppled, and new systems of social class and economics emerged. Humanity is again at the tipping point. Like the printing press, digital devices connected to the Internet are unequivocal game changers.

THE VAN METER STORY

Beginning in the fall of 2009, the Van Meter Community School District began utilizing social media tools to create a global footprint, becoming leaders in transforming teaching and learning.

The Van Meter Community School District is located in Central Iowa, just outside the capital city of Des Moines. It is a small district of about 630 students in grades kindergarten through twelfth grade. North of Van Meter, growing at a rate of almost 600 students a year, is the Waukee Community School District. The West Des Moines School District—boasting an Olympic Gold medalist and *Dancing With the Stars* champion, Shawn Johnson, as well as a Grammy-winning music program and state championship athletic teams among its assets—lies to the east. To the west and south are several "county seat" school districts, which are three times larger than Van Meter.

Thus surrounded by prosperous communities with growing school districts, Van Meter was facing an identity crisis. The real fear was that Van Meter would experience either rapid uncontrollable growth like that happening in Waukee and/or no growth at all; that it would cease to exist, and be swallowed up by one of the neighboring districts. In both cases, the fear was that the district was not in control of its own destiny. With that fear came a sense of urgency and a realization of the need for change. To ensure survivability and viability, new thinking was needed.

The need for change came from the realization that the current system of education is broken. At present, education in the

United States is a century-old design, as outlined in Chapter 2. At the beginning of the Industrial Revolution, our country moved away from "rugged individualism" to interdependent global consumerism. System thinking at that time was applied to learning design, and the United States moved from the one-room schoolhouse to the consolidated factory model school system. That model served us well for more than 100 years, but the world has since changed. The crucial need for the United States today is an educational system that empowers students and develops creativity and imagination, not one focused on standardization and conformity. A new system of learning that is differentiated and that connects to student passions and strengths must be made a reality. Teaching and learning need to transform to something yet undefined.

New Thinking Emerges

Recognizing that the educational system was flawed and failing had ramifications. Bringing this to local patrons was a challenge. In many instances, elements of the school community did not see the need, and in some instances, resisted change. Information electronically provided to patrons and stakeholders in real time quickened the realization that change was needed and was inevitable. Crucial to the transformation was a focus on learning and an acknowledgement of the world our children live in, including its technology and social media.

In the fall of 2009, all students in Grades 7–12 were issued laptop computers in Van Meter. In 2010, sixth graders were included, making Van Meter a sixth-to-twelfth-grade "1-to-1" laptop district. For teachers, this meant developing pedagogy to use technology to enhance and amplify learning. This change not only led to significant changes in teaching and learning, but also in how Van Meter would begin to leverage social media tools to tell its story and form a new standard for public relations.

John acknowledged the fact that the transformation of the Van Meter School District required some significant changes.

Van Meter's direction going forward was to embrace change and build capacity within the organization to make transformation possible. Using e-mail to send out weekly administrative updates kept stakeholders informed of the progress being made. YouTube videos, blogs, and weekly updates responded to and addressed the conditions and emotions generated from change. Without the systematic use of social media as part of a greater public relations effort, stakeholder embracement of these dramatic changes might not have materialized, and this, in turn, might have derailed the transformation of this school district.

Through the efforts of Secondary Principal Deron Durflinger, Director of Teaching and Learning Jen Sigrist, Teacher Librarian Shannon Miller, and District Technology Director Mike Linde, social media were used to connect and tell the Van Meter story. They shared their thinking and progress in designing a new modality of learning using technology. Utilizing blogs, wikis, YouTube, and Twitter, the team built professional learning networks in order to share and grow, as well as to model that behavior for staff. Through social media, synchronicity occurred. Others shared in the findings Van Meter unearthed. In creating the #vanmeter brand, thousands connected through Twitter. As ideas and concepts were shared virtually, they affirmed that the present education system was broken.

Get Connected, Tell the Story, and Do Not Walk Alone

Because of its size and proximity to Des Moines, Van Meter had little access or coverage by the media. With the exception of monthly "Bulldog Brief" school newsletters and the school Web page, Van Meter was isolated. Social media would become the means by which Van Meter would share information with patrons in real time and connect regionally, nationally, and globally. Social media, specifically Twitter, gave Van Meter schools a voice and connections not only to stakeholders but also to educators, politicians, inventors, and business leaders regionally and nationally. Through social media and Web 2.0 tools, classrooms moved from being silos of learning to global learning centers. The Van Meter School District's future now had unlimited potential (Carver, 2013).

The Van Meter story teaches us a powerful lesson: If we do not tell our story, someone else will. Unfortunately, more often than not, the story that is told about schools is negative and ignores the many great things happening within and beyond the walls. The goal of mainstream media is to increase viewers, ratings, and circulation. When it comes to education, the stories that most often help the media improve their bottom line are those with a negative spin. In a time of unprecedented education reform efforts and relentless attacks on the profession, leaders no longer have to stand by and take the relentless onslaught of a negative press.

Digital leadership is about building the capacity to create a solid foundation for positive public relations using social media that complements communication efforts, as described in Chapter 5. It empowers leaders to become the storytellers in-chief and, in turn, creates a constant flow of information that highlights and focuses on schoolwide success and positive culture. This makes total sense as not only a cost-saving pathway to sharing positive news, but also a practical means to get this information into the hands of stakeholders who frequently rely on and use tools such as Twitter, Facebook, YouTube, and many others.

SOCIAL MEDIA TOOLS FOR PUBLIC RELATIONS

Social media integration for public relations should no longer be optional for schools. Whereas its use for communication provides basic information in a timely fashion, digital leaders take it to another level by crafting specific, positive messages. Social media allow leaders to create unique communities for their schools/districts, establish a digital presence, construct feedback mechanisms on websites and other spaces, and welcome stakeholders into a conversation. Upon becoming principal of New Milford High School in June of 2007, I made it one of my primary goals to work hard at sharing all of the accomplishments centered around teaching and learning occurring with my stakeholders on a routine basis. As principal, I was aware of these things, but I was pretty sure that the majority of the educational community was not. Combined with the fact that the local media were finicky when it came to reporting on the many positive things occurring at my school (or any school, for that matter), I decided that it was up to me to take control of our public relations.

It was at this point that I created the monthly "Principal's Report" that can be viewed on the main page of our high school website. Even though it is simplistic from an aesthetic standpoint, this document is a powerhouse when it comes to the depth of information that it contains. Then social media came into my life. My immersion in Twitter made me realize that I could take my public relations plan to a whole new level. As I learned about still other social media tools, I began to diversify the types of information shared and how it was disseminated. This necessitated the creation of a media waiver in order to share information related to students (Appendix C). I have implemented the following digital leadership public relations that look like this:

- Principal's Report or District Newsletter: A monthly summary of achievements and advancements that have a positive impact on teacher, learning, and school culture. This can be a stand-alone document on a school website or something more dynamic, such as a blog. The benefits of having this information in a blog format are that it encourages stakeholder engagement, since readers can comment on the posts.
- Twitter: Daily updates on news, events, student achievements, staff innovations, etc. It is also another medium to distribute the Principal's Report. Capturing moments through pictures, video, and text as they happen has proven to be a powerful method of improving a school's public relations plan as stakeholders receive

this information at home or on the go through mobile devices.

- Facebook page: This serves the same purpose as a school Twitter account, but this tool has much more influence, as many more students, parents, and alumni utilize Facebook on a daily basis. In addition to school-generated material, public relations efforts are maximized when links to mainstream news articles are added to its page. Once established, a link to the Facebook page can be placed on the school website.
- Picture tools: Flickr, Picasa, and Instagram provide leaders with the ability to share and showcase students, staff, and events through pictures. Separate accounts can be set up just for the school.
- Video tools: Well-known tools such as YouTube and Vimeo allow leaders to share and showcase students, staff, and events through video. YouTube is great for video clips of around ten minutes or less, while Vimeo will support larger video uploads. Separate accounts can be created just for schools to post entire events such as concerts or athletic competitions, or to highlight montages created using popular technology tools such as iMovie. Many schools across the country are now creating promotional videos and trailers using iMovie as a part of their public relations plans. The ability to shoot video from iPhones and iPads and easily create short videos using available templates has become a hallmark for digital leaders anticipating how to better engage their stakeholders. One last video tool is Ustream, a free service that allows leaders to stream live video and archive it to share at a later time. This can be used to make events such as graduation, guest speakers, athletics, musical productions, and concerts available to a greater audience.
- Blogs: There is no better tool for sharing detailed student and staff accomplishments. They allow for detailed descriptions of classroom innovations, summaries of school events, descriptions of large construction

projects, student guest posts, and state-of-the-school/ district messages. Most important, they allow leaders to tell their good stories. Multimedia content such as video, images, and audio can be seamlessly integrated to create a more engaging experience for stakeholders. As leaders become more tech savvy, each blogging tool offers specialized widgets to customize the blog. Widgets enable bloggers to modify the design and content of their blogs without any HTML knowledge. The three most popular platforms are Google Blogger, Wordpress, and Typepad.

EDUCATION TRANSFORMATION: TELLING THE STORY OF RURAL AREAS

Educational transformation is occurring throughout the state of Iowa, with rural areas facing many of the same challenges of urban areas. Population shifts, shrinking populations, how to prepare youth for the twenty-first century, and jobs are all common themes. Rural Iowa also faces the challenge of connectivity and providing course offerings. The Howard-Winneshiek Community School District is a community of 1,300 students located in rural Northeastern Iowa that now has John Carver at the helm. With elementary campuses located in Elma, Lime Springs, and Cresco, and junior high and high school campuses also in Cresco, the district is spread out over 462 square miles. The district's mission statement, "To prepare and empower our students to think creatively, serve, contribute, and succeed locally and globally," illustrates the community's commitment.

In July 2012, the Howard-Winneshiek Community School District established the #2020HowardWinn brand on Twitter to enhance its public relations. The year 2020 is when the current fifth grade will graduate. The goal of the district is that by 2020, a new educational system will be in place. This new system of learning would identify student passions and strengths, then utilize social media and Web 2.0 tools to differentiate instruction, connect learners, and create. A strategic outcome is for students to develop their imagination. Supports and protocols will be established to support young entrepreneurs.

Recently, iPads have been issued to sixth, seventh, and eighth graders, and SMART Boards have been placed in all classrooms. Digital devices will be in the hands of high school students in the winter of 2013. Twitter, e-mail, and text messages are being used to notify stakeholders of school delays and closings due to weather. The Howard-Winneshiek Board of Education is on Twitter and follows district happenings. Iowa Lt. Governor Kim Reynolds has shared that she follows #2020HowardWinn tweets. Skype, iChat, and Google I are being used to provide real-time video connections. This is, in turn, facilitating differentiated instruction and learning projects between Howard-Winn elementary classrooms and the world. *The Weekly Administrative Update* is sent out electronically to stakeholders, and the district has created its own YouTube channel.

All of these social media efforts have connected a small, rural community with the rest of Iowa and beyond. For rural communities like this one, social media is the best tool for public relations. These communities finally have a voice and are telling their stories. Howard-Winneshiek is participating and providing leadership at the regional and state level for the Governor's Science, Technology, Engineering and Math (STEM) initiative. Partnering with Northeast Iowa Community College (NICC) with support from Keystone Area Education Association, the district is moving rapidly to build a K–12 STEM talent pipeline. Howard-Winn Board of Education President Duane Bodermann's desire is to "position the Howard-Winneshiek schools as the educational destination for the region," and board member James Kitchen's belief that "it's all about quality service" sums it all up. Because of this thinking, the rate of change at Howard-Winneshiek is accelerating exponentially. The biggest challenge facing Howard-Winn and rural Iowa is obtaining broadband connectivity. There are large gaps in coverage across Iowa, and this must be addressed in order to continue to move forward.

As leaders begin to integrate social media tools into their public relations plans, they will begin the process of making their schools more transparent and they will evolve into the role of storyteller-in-chief. This transparency will give stakeholders a clearer picture of all of the many positive things taking place each and every day. Each tool listed above should be linked to current school websites. URLs should be added to all print materials and e-mail signatures in order to maximize exposure to these sources of information. In time, a greater sense of pride will develop, as stakeholders will be more knowledgeable about the great work being done.

Summary

Historically, the ability to share thinking and perspective has been limited to those who had money and was subject to filters and "editors." These "screens" determined what ideas and thoughts went forward. Digital devices connected to the Internet and utilizing social network tools have leveled the playing field. Today, any person, any age, anywhere, at any time can connect with any person, any age, anywhere, at any time to share thinking and create, and the outcomes are "going viral." We are truly no longer "I" but "we."

7

Branding

Communication and public relations can be treated as two different entities or as two essential leadership strategies that work in concert with one another. Digital leaders seize on the latter while building a powerful brand presence for their institutions and/or leadership style. Trish Rubin knows branding matters in a changing world of learning fueled by powerful digital resources. She presents one simple definition of brand that connects with your innovative role as an educational manager in a digital world: *Brand is a distinctive sum experience people have with a product or service.* Whether they know it or not, leaders who have integrated social media as a component of their communications and public relations strategies have already begun the process of establishing a brand presence. Digital leadership focuses on behaviors and specific strategies that will create a positive brand presence, which, in turn, will instill a greater sense of pride in the leaders' work and/or school function.

From her own journey, Trish knows school leaders are responsible for the sum experience people have with educational products and services. She believes professional conversations about developing, delivering, and maintaining excellence can be enriched with two discussion topics on

Brand-ed, her own educationalist view of branding that fuses the brand concept with education. Trish Rubin, MA, MGA, stands at the intersection of a life in education with an encore career in business. Her résumé is one of a teacher, school administrator, and national literacy thought leader. Today, Trish's business calling card identifies her as a business brand strategist, but she has the heart of an educator and takes every chance to blend her experience in schools with her communication work in business.

THE BUSINESS OF *BRAND-ED*: SCHOOL CULTURE, STUDENT ACHIEVEMENT, AND RESOURCING

Trish's career path leads me to wonder, "Can a smart school manager use a business concept to inform educational practice in a digital world?" Her answer is yes. In her vision, *Brand-ed* school reform conversations are led, not by a Madison Avenue executive, but by a progressive school leader possessing digital tools and an interest in a brand's benefit to three educational outcomes: *school culture, student achievement,* and *school funding/resourcing.* She has seen instructional managers quickly build and communicate distinctive educational "products and services" using elements of a *Brand-ed* campaign, and forecasts that more educational leaders will choose this actionable path. The digital world empowers leaders across an expanding social media landscape to do so. Despite the public school Common Core and the argument that educational change happens at a glacial pace, a digital school leader can create unique brand value to support excellence as seamlessly as the ad men and women of yesterday, and without the three-martini lunches! This can be accomplished both at the school and on the individual professional level.

From her office in New York City, Trish made her connection with me serendipitously as I was building my school's visibility on a nightly news broadcast, one of the benefits of exciting opportunities for my school through the business of my own *Brand-ed* thinking (Rubin, 2013).

Why *Brand-ed* Thinking? A Look at Brand History

Brand-ed may be Trish's new term, but branding isn't a new concept. Decanters of wine found in the ruins of Pompeii attest to early "labeling" of product. Today, brand impacts politics and purchasing. *Passion* is Spain's one-word "nation brand," according to UK brand theorist Wally Olins (2008). Nation branding is a science that sells, and it is similar to the science of branding the next popular children's toy. Big returns are at stake in both efforts. You think the word *brand* is overused? That's the power of a word on digital steroids. The brand conversation is everywhere. This pervasive *B* word is no longer restricted to corporate marketing meetings.

Early in the twentieth century, the Morton Salt girl and the Quaker Oats man heralded the birth of mass brand presence in the marketplace. In the 1960s, brand moved beyond packaging. *Mad Men* executives created product "personalities." The Marlboro Man and the Maytag Repair Man built relationships with the consumer through the "social media" driver of the day, the color television. Madison Avenue's separate advertising teams and creative departments merged, giving birth to the science of brand building. You can argue that today's products and services are sold online in a blink, no creative team necessary, but the real science of knowing how to *successfully* brand remains a form of art. This is strategic, not magical thinking.

In our twenty-first century, brand building isn't limited to the *Mad Men* crowd. Brand thinking—building compelling missions and campaigns—is possible for millions who own computers or smartphones. When digital parents in your school community develop Web pages for the unborn, complete with naming campaigns, they are launching a personal brand. Despite some of the laughable misuses, the concept is a still a serious component of business—and can be for education. Your community is plugged in digitally and is already impacting your institutional brand, for better or worse. Like Trish, digital leaders see the inherent value of establishing a brand presence in today's world.

Historically, brand is based on building relationships, and relationships are key to brand campaigning in education. Aren't educators always building, brokering, and sustaining relationships? With a *Brand-ed* mindset, "initiating" relationships becomes a first step. Strategic brand is grown through mutual trust and good faith as you strategically initiate new connections. You can grow your own professional brand personality as well as that of your institution by purposefully creating relationships that lead to school improvement.

Two Conversations Around *Brand-ed* Thinking

Trish suggests two *Brand-ed* conversations to test the thinking about bringing a business marketing concept to your school:

1. The one about your professional brand

2. The one about your school's brand

The first conversation is reflective. It's about developing your own brand, not to celebrity star level, but one that creates a leadership personality to spark new professional effectiveness. The second conversation is shared with the community. Introduce it to *Brand-ed* thinking and the idea of delivering on a promise of excellence for educational "product and service." Once you have sorted out your professional personality and begin to live it across the digital landscape, teaching your own stakeholders makes you as creative as any Madison Avenue marketer.

Conversation One: Professional Brand

Ask yourself, Do I need a professional brand? With an eye on the growing digital world, Trish believes the answer is yes. You need what business guru Tom Peters (1999) calls a Brand YOU—one that is based on a core belief. It's what you stand for and who you are. As in nation building, reduce it to a word and run with it. CBS journalist Lee Woodruff the wife of the nearly fatally injured reporter Bob Woodruff, has a personal brand of RESILIENCE, and all her work and relationships are informed by that one word. If you want to build a *Brand-ed* conversation, start with your own brand-naming project.

Call it a personal brand, call it a professional brand, or your brand personality. Live it. Become the manager of purposeful, visible behaviors that initiate and build relationships and connections, both face to face and in social media. This kind of professional brand does not have to be personally transparent. It should communicate, but it does not have to be intrusive. You don't have to share your favorite color or where you spent last summer as you build your brand on social media spaces such as LinkedIn, Facebook, Instragram, Google+, and Twitter.

Take a page from business. Think USP, *unique selling proposition*. Think Volvo, whose famous USP is "Safety." Volvo sells safety in a word. Your own brand is a genuine sell. You may already have a strong sense of personal brand if you are part of the digital landscape, but if you've shied away because social media seems to be an "all-about-me" effort, get beyond that. This isn't egocentric behavior; it's leadership survival in a digital world of messaging and a means to an educational end. Be the CEO, Chief Education Officer, of your brand effort. This effort creates loyalty and trust, the kind that made mega brands like Apple and Starbucks successful with their market.

If you don't intentionally claim your brand, some stakeholder on the other end of a computer will do it for you. Take charge of digital and real-time presence. You can build the institutional brand upon your solid foundation. Think about who can help you create a powerful brand presence. For me, it was Trish Rubin, and we have been engaged in dynamic conversations about the place of branding in my professional development. She suggests starting your *Brand-ed* mission with her acronym, be a *"Brand-ed* Ace." Digital leadership drives leaders to develop their own brand, which happens as they interact in online spaces through the use of social media tools. These interactions define one's thoughts, beliefs, and opinions on education and leadership. They also provide examples of work, ideas, awards, and other types of recognition. All of these combined form an educational brand presence.

When you know your brand, associate, create, and engage. Make yourself visible by choosing to associate with communities in real time and online as you initiate relationships. Create interest around what you do and say and the content you share with those communities. Finally, engage digitally and face to face with partners to acquire resources and discover opportunity in your effort. Trish advances the best minds in the field for leaders to study, such as books and blogs by Keith Ferazzi, Tom Peters, Brian Solis, and Dan Schwabel. Through the work of these individuals, leaders can mine the personal branding conversation of thousands of people, and not just marketers and salespeople. Brand is a professional fit. Face it. Educators are in the sales business. Trish speaks of how as a teacher she sold the value of education to kids, parents, bosses, other teachers, and businesses. How much easier it would be now with a clear personal brand in place?

Ask yourself, What's the return? Trish sees the *Brand-ed* "collision'" of business thinking and education as a powerful opportunity for leaders to create a new, more engaging presence. No more ivory towers. Thomas Friedman (2005), author of *The World Is Flat*, calls this an "imagination mash-up—" that is, thinking that combines business and education in a dynamic way. A *Brand-ed* leader expands relationships with business and education partners for better schools. A professional brand creates the ROI—what business calls a Return on Investment. This investment yields institutional return through improved school culture, school performance, and school resources.

Conversation Two: School Brand

Does leadership brand impact school culture? You've created your relational brand. Connect it to school improvement. Communicate brand promise for improving your school's culture, achievement, and resourcing. Trish sees these first discussions around school culture. Ask your team how you are communicating your brand to the community. Your innovative thinking signals exciting change for your team. Encourage them to examine their own. Ferriter, Ramsden, and Sheninger (2011) identified the following factors that go into a school's brand:

- Student Achievement: Standardized test scores are most often used to evaluate the overall effectiveness of a school. Public relations and communication efforts focused on growth evidence in this area can be conveyed through social media. Doing so will help to create and strengthen a school's brand presence.
- Quality of Teachers and Administrators: Student achievement is directly linked to the quality of the staff at a school. Stakeholders are often more than willing to move to towns with higher taxes that attract the best and brightest educators. Utilizing social media to convey staff statistics can build the confidence of any community, which has a positive impact on a school's brand.
- Innovative Instructional Practices and Programs: Course offerings, curricular decisions, unique programs, and innovative instructional practices play a key role in student engagement while having a positive impact on student outcomes (Whitehurst, 2009). Schools that have unique course offerings, curricula, and programs make a school or district stand out. The publication and dissemination of this information sends a powerful message related to college and career readiness and the ability of students to follow their passions.
- Extracurricular Activities: Extracurricular activities are a valued component of any school community and help to develop well-rounded students. Leaders who use social media as part of a combined communications and public relations strategy will not only spotlight these activities, but also gain the attention of stakeholders.

Extend the conversation to include institutional brand and recruit an invested community. Private schools have long flourished under institutional branding. Today, social media, word-of-mouth, and conversational marketing digital tools can quickly build identity that took private schools years to build. All K–12 schools, public and private, can use digital strategies to establish a brand to build a following just as private schools have done for years through traditional means. Your "market" is the entire community of stakeholders. Engage them in a Madison Avenue strategy that creates a pervasive school culture to unify, create excellence, and attract followers who want to take part in the brand of your school.

Ask your community members if they want to go beyond the logo to a brand of school achievement. Encourage thinking beyond a logo, a mascot, and a typical educator mission statement to build visible signals of *Brand-ed.* Study your school's mission statement with a new eye on marketing. That's the first public signal of change. What makes your Web-page mission statement different from any other school that offers value to stakeholders? Does it inspire trust? Suggest a deep belief in what the school is about? Microsoft's Bill Gates knew what he was about. His company's vision statement for thirty years was simple: "A computer on every desk."

Tie the threads of existing efforts for school achievement together. Anchor them as *"Brand-ed* conversations" for achievement. As you lead your community, look toward funding/resourcing possibilities. With a brand campaign, the words *student achievement* become authentic. Not achievement for the sake of a number on a test report, but achievement that is reflected by the authentic culture of learning that the school demonstrates every single day.

Digital leadership is about making your community a part of new school resourcing through brand building. Trish talks about the "1,000-people-who-know-you" rule in mass marketing as a guide for your campaign. As you begin, focus effort on serving a small part of the market and keep them happy. Your most loyal fans are already with you. As you begin to tell your own brand story through social media and digital contacts, these people will be your biggest supporters, and they will initiate more to the cause. Identify your core group. Create the movement with these cheerleaders.

Marketing isn't really a new concept for schools that have benefited from limited word of mouth and sporadic public relations in the local daily paper. In your *Brand-ed* initiative, however, digital marketing—that is, communicating with wider audiences about school product or service—is innovative and sustaining. In the digital world, your supporters could be sitting down the street or 8,000 miles away. Engage them with the same marketing messages that keep them supportive. Promoting the school brand gets the word out about school culture and achievement. Your campaign can attract and retain people who care about education. Just think how many more budgets would be approved if the school brand were marketed more strongly and more personally every day.

When Trish Rubin gets excited about branding, it is because she sees its unique possibilities for school resourcing and funding. Imagine the intellect, talent, and means that your graduates hold and the marketing opportunities they present. Share the brand with alumni. Engage them with your current stakeholders. Most of your graduates live online, so virtually campaign to welcome them home and share the educational experience you are building with parents, students, and community. Bringing back graduates through a marketing campaign of social media and direct word of mouth can make a difference in getting financial and community resources of all kinds for your school. Both school branding conversations can be summarized in Table 7.1.

SUMMARY

In a word, persevere. Let business-branding history inspire you to make your own *Brand-ed* history. To be a brand ACE in a digital world takes patience, but the returns are there for you and your school stakeholders. The creation and maintenance of a brand presence rely on the consistent and targeted use of social media for school communications and public relations. When combined with traditional methods, a leader's and

Table 7.1   *Brand-ed* School Leadership

Brand-ed Identity			
	Positioning	*Vision*	*Personality*
Build	Where do I stand as an educator? • My values • My unique perspective	How I use my brand to benefit: • School culture • Student achievement • Funding • Resourcing	What's my unique selling proposition (USP)? • One word that illustrates my *Brand-ed* view for my community
Brand-ed Pillars of Action (ACE—Associate, Create, Engage)			
	Associate	*Create*	*Engage*
Share	• Become relational. • Join diverse communities. • Support groups. • Balance real-time with online connections. • Choose causes that reflect your brand.	• See yourself as a product. • Market your value across communities. • Develop real-time and online interests. • Create and share content. • Present yourself as thought leader.	• Be transparent to your comfort level. • Join daily conversations online and in real time. • Be a connector of others. • Give before you get.

Source: Copyright © Trish Rubin (2013, March). Adapted with permission.
www.trishnyc.com

school's brand will be established and resonate throughout the school and education community. The resulting message will inform and promote all the positive aspects of leadership, education, and established school culture. Leaders in a digital world understand and embrace lessons from the private sector to better connect and engage with all stakeholders in the twenty-first century.

8

Professional Growth and Development

A SHIFT IN PROFESSIONAL LEARNING

Serving as an educational administrator is an exceptionally rewarding profession; however, it can also be an extraordinarily challenging one. Administrators will be the first to admit "it's lonely at the top." Principals and central office administrators often feel isolated in their roles. As both leaders and managers of their organizations, they are expected to be everything to everyone. From teacher supervision to student discipline to curriculum development to change management, principals and other school leaders need to continually develop themselves professionally in numerous areas. Traditional professional development offerings for principals are often lacking in their approach to developing comprehensive leaders, and they offer little to no opportunity for school leaders to work collaboratively and network with one another. It is essential for principals and school leaders to develop professional learning networks both within and beyond their local organizations. With today's technologies able to connect people around the world more efficiently than ever, school leaders can easily amass ideas and support structures in order to better themselves and bring a wealth of resources to their schools.

As a first-year principal, Lyn Hilt quickly recognized the need to reach out to other administrators for support, ideas, and feedback. Though her administrative colleagues at the local level were generous in their offerings of support, Lyn's desire to lead her elementary school and support her teachers and students in twenty-first-century teaching and learning required that she reach beyond the walls of her school building to access the expertise of school administrators and teachers from around the world.

It started simply enough. Lyn turned to the Internet to explore topics of interest, including professional learning communities (PLCs), classroom management, home/school communications, educational technology, and teacher supervision and evaluation. While Lyn found relevant information in educational journals and formal publications, she soon realized that many educators chose to share their personal, real-world educational experiences with others through blogging. Lyn recognized the value of writing as a means of reflection in order to better her practice and appreciated that others did the same. To organize the growing list of blogs she enjoyed, she utilized Google Reader to make reading a streamlined effort.

Lyn decided she would like to begin blogging to share her ideas with the global education community. Initially, her blog contained no information identifying her or her school. Like many educators who first contemplate sharing their ideas online, she was fearful of receiving negative or critical feedback. She wrote simple summaries of topics of interest to her as an administrator, posing questions about how to approach problem solving or program implementation. Lyn's earliest blog posts served their purpose in helping her reflect upon her practice, but her audience was limited. Most of the questions posed in her posts remained unanswered, unlike other blogs she read where meaningful conversations erupted in the comments sections. She needed a way to efficiently share her posts and grow her readership in order to deepen the conver-sations and her learning.

THE RISE OF SOCIAL MEDIA AS A TOOL FOR GROWTH AND PROFESSIONAL DEVELOPMENT

At an educational technology conference in 2007, Lyn was first introduced to the social networking tool, Twitter. She created an account initially but did not interact with other educators, instead convincing herself Twitter was a tool best used for fol-lowing celebrity happenings and for people who thought it was fun to share what they ate for breakfast that day with the world. Through her reading of educational blogs, however, Lyn noticed that many of her favorite bloggers shared their posts via Twitter. So, in 2009, she began to become more active on Twitter, following other principals and teachers whose voices were prevalent in conversations about the topics she cared so much about. She discovered a weekly Twitter chat for educators, #edchat, and through her participation, she began to develop professional relationships with educators from around the world. She tweeted links to her blog posts and soon discovered that more comments and enriched conversa-tions about teaching and learning emerged.

While she was at first fearful of putting herself "out there," Lyn now understood the importance of transparency in learn-ing in online networks. Lyn's blog, The Principal's Posts (lynhilt.com), was becoming well read, and she was gaining access to the resources, ideas, and feedback that she needed to grow professionally. Through her blogging and tweeting efforts, she connected with other principals such as George Couros (@gcouros) and Patrick Larkin (@patrickmlarkin), and became a contributor on Connected Principals (connectedprincipals .com), a blog featuring posts from principals and school lead-ers around the world. She was grateful to find a community of administrators who viewed themselves as "learners first" (Hilt, 2013).

Personal Learning Networks (PLNs)

Lyn's use of Twitter was one of the integral steps in her developing a Personal Learning Network (PLN). PLNs can be defined as collections of like-minded people with whom one exchanges information and engages in conversation. These conversations focus on mutual interests and goals, with the main objective of professional growth and improvement. They have been around for centuries and originally consisted of friends, family, coworkers, etc. The evolution of the Internet and social media has changed the dynamics of PLN formation, but they still serve the same centuries-old purpose. Free social networking tools and seemingly ubiquitous access to them provide leaders with the ability to connect and learn like never before. What used to be boundaries to PLN formation—time, location, access to people—are no longer issues.

Educators have always understood the value of collaboration and, as a result, professional communities of practice arose. The research of Alec Couros (2006) illustrates the differences between educators that are and are not connected through social networks and identifies the shift needed to move from a traditional teacher to a networked approach. He describes how networks found in our traditional schools are more closed than open. An educator may have professional and social contacts that span the globe, but these are likely rare. Teacher practice and content knowledge are more likely shaped by geography than by digital connectedness. This is how learning communities have been structured for many, many years. The flow of information and resources also tends to be more one-dimensional (Figure 8.1).

Technology has changed everything when it comes to professional learning. A connected leader is still supported by traditional networks but now has the ability to tap into other professional learning resources using digital tools. Beyond the usual localized relations, those who are connected to a greater social network are more informed about their practice, beliefs, and perceptions regarding education. Perhaps more important,

Figure 8.1   Traditionally Networked Educator

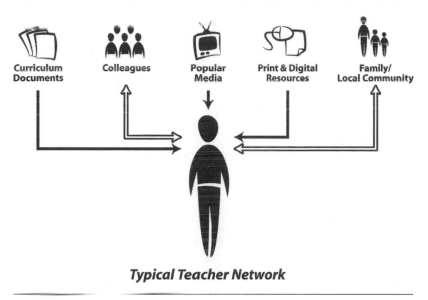

Typical Teacher Network

Source: Couros, A. (2006). Used with permission.

these educators engage in both *consumption* and *publication.* Knowledge is shared and exchanged, not simply taken.

The driving force in a connected learning model is each individual leader. Each member of a PLN transitions between the physical and virtual networks to communicate, collaborate, acquire resources, elicit feedback, get support, and share ideas, data, strategies, and information. It is the consistent give and take at the individual level that makes a collective PLN exponentially stronger, more knowledgeable, and wiser. Why would any leader refuse the opportunity to tap into this human-generated portal of information and to improve? The essence of the PLN is that the *who* of potential members and collaborators is increased exponentially because of individual members networking through collaborative technology platforms, the *what* (Jacobs, 2009).

This dynamic model of learning not only supports the diverse needs of leaders, but also emphasizes a two-way flow of information (Figure 8.2).

Figure 8.2   Digital Leaders

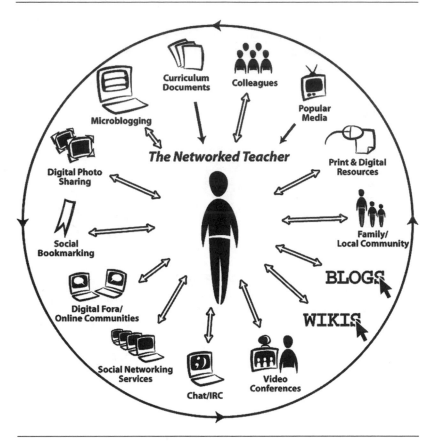

Source: Couros, A. (2006). Used with permission.

Lyn Hilt was now able to quickly acquire quality resources to support her leadership efforts. Lyn was able to reach out to members of her network when in need of feedback, encouragement, and inspiration. In addition to the principalship, Lyn served as the elementary technology integrator in her small district and was charged with leading educational technology initiatives at the elementary level. This required her to become more informed about twenty-first-century teaching and learning. She was asked to write elementary-student blogging guidelines in order to proceed with the district's new blogging initiative. Rather than begin from scratch, potentially spending hours of time on the task, Lyn tweeted a request for examples of current student blogging guidelines that other educators were using. Within minutes, she received a tweet with the link to a quality set of guidelines developed by a fellow educator. Within a short time, Lyn modified the contents to meet her district's needs, credited the teacher who created the original guidelines, and the task was complete. Another challenge for any principal is supporting teachers of various grade levels and content areas. Lyn used Twitter and her PLN's knowledge base to acquire resources for her teachers at all levels, including lesson ideas, research studies and articles, and tech tools for use in the classroom. She encouraged her teachers to develop their own PLNs, and she supported her teachers in that effort by modeling her use of social media to form connections with other educators. She also held workshops for teachers to help them learn more about social media and the power of the PLN. Soon her teachers were reaching out and forming their own PLNs via Twitter, connecting with grade-level colleagues from around the world. They were leading technology initiatives in the district, forming global classroom partnerships through the use of programs such as Skype and Edmodo, sharing their ideas with one another more freely, and ultimately enhancing student learning experiences in their classrooms.

Through the support of her PLN, Lyn became more knowledgeable about twenty-first-century teaching and learning. She was able to enhance communication and collaborative opportunities in her school. The use of Google Docs and blogs streamlined the way she communicated with her teachers, and many of her teachers embraced the use of these tools to plan more collaboratively in teams. To strengthen home/school connections, she began communicating with parents frequently through the use of a school blog and Facebook page, replacing traditional paper newsletters that did not allow for two-way communication. Her community was given access to the school's happenings with one click.

Parents had the option to engage with the content she shared, such as commenting on posts and viewing photos from school events. She transformed the way she approached professional development at her school, thanks to the philosophies and ideas shared by those in her PLN. Through her engagement with online learning networks, Lyn received opportunities to present "the power of the PLN" to other educators at local, state, and national education conferences. She became involved with organizations such as Powerful Learning Practice and enjoyed being challenged each day to transform teaching and learning not only at her school, but by influencing other educators around the world.

"It's hard to describe how great the impact of my PLN has been," Lyn states. "I am definitely a changed leader because of the connections and relationships I've formed. There's nothing like needing support or an idea and reaching out to hundreds, even thousands, of other educators for feedback. I've been introduced to ideas and content I never would have learned through traditional professional development. Forming a PLN is a necessity for any school leader who wishes to grow professionally."

Connectedness as the Standard

Digital leadership requires connectedness as an essential component to cultivate innovative practices and lead sustainable change. It is not an option, but a standard and professional obligation. The power and value of a connected learning model are tough to ignore. Leaders become the epicenter of their learning and determine *what, where,* and *when* they want to learn. This makes the learning process meaningful, relevant, applicable, and convenient. With these structures in place, the foundation is established to unleash passion, creativity, and a pursuit of innovation to do what we do better. Connectedness and control of learning provide leaders with the ability to determine their own path and to differentiate to meet their diverse learning needs.

This type of learning is fueled by intrinsic motivation, which is the most pivotal ingredient essential to lifelong learning, growth, innovation, and sustainable change. Passion and interest drive this model of learning, which in itself becomes a self-sustaining entity. Connectedness provides unparalleled access to a wealth of free resources. Using tools to share and acquire resources expands each leader's horizons. Many educators don't even know what tools exist, let alone how they can enhance the teaching and learning process. The knowledge in this area is typically even less for leaders. Where traditional models of professional growth and development fall short, a PLN driven by connections and conversations fills in the gaps.

It is a two-way mechanism for constructive feedback, support, and advice. This feature alone is priceless. No longer do leaders need to feel like they inhabit isolated islands in their respective positions. Distance boundaries and budgetary challenges are overcome with just a device, Internet connection, and a desire to improve. Stand-along silos of information, the cultural components of many schools and leaders, dissipate. There need no longer be a quest to reinvent the wheel and constantly develop new, fresh ideas, because some of the best ideas and proven strategies for school and leadership improvement are readily available and accessible through a PLN.

There is no cost for this powerful opportunity to grow. All it costs is an investment of time, which we ultimately determine. Leaders who embrace a digital style understand that this investment is necessary to create the types of schools needed to prepare students for a digital world. To accomplish this lofty goal, leaders must put in the time to learn in a way that drives them. This will then set the stage to build capacity in others through knowledge gained from a global network.

It provides the means to connect with the best minds in the field of education. One of the most amazing attributes associated with social media is that they make the world a much smaller place. You can now connect with world-renowned educational researchers or experts from your living room. Possibly even more powerful is the ability to learn from actual practitioners doing the same job as you. Accessibility to these ideas, strategies, and collective knowledge from both of these groups will ultimately make you a better educator. Silos of information become a thing of the past. A connected learning model is also extremely transparent.

A PLN will provide leaders with the seeds of change, but it is up to each respective leader to plant and cultivate them in order to witness their growth and development into transformative culture elements. If he or she does, it will not be long before these seeds of change mature and begin to bear fruit by becoming embedded, sustainable components of the school culture and professional growth. With the tools that are now available, connectedness should be the standard, not just an option in education. When reflecting upon the many benefits of becoming connected, digital leaders understand that they cannot afford not to become connected.

Developing a PLN

No one can argue that the evolution of the real-time Web has dramatically altered how we communicate, gather information, and reflect. The construction of a PLN enables leaders to harness the power inherent in twenty-first-century technologies in order to create a professional growth tool that is accessible whenever and wherever necessary. In particular, a PLN will provide any leader with a constant supply of resources, thought-provoking discussions, knowledge, leadership strategies, and ways to successfully integrate technology.

Most leaders have no idea where to begin when attempting to create a PLN that meets their learning and leadership needs. The vast majority don't even possess a working knowledge of basic Web 2.0 tools and how they can be utilized for teaching and learning. The following list (Ferriter, Ramsden, & Sheninger, 2011) provides some good PLN starting points and resources to assist any leader in a digital world who desires to take his or her professional growth to new levels.

- Twitter (twitter.com): Microblogging platform that allows educators from all corners of the globe to communicate in 140 characters or less and allows for the sharing of resources, discussion of best practices, and collaboration. Twitter chats are a fantastic way to connect with and learn from practicing administrators. One great example is #Satchat. Founded by Brad Currie (@bcurrie5) and Scott Rocco (@scottrrocco), #Satchat takes place every Saturday morning on Twitter and enables educators from around the world to connect and share best practices that will inevitably promote the success of all students. The inspiration for this Twitter discussion directly relates to my work and that of others who promote what is possible when social media and Web tools are effectively utilized. The charge of improving every day as a lead learner and having substantial influence on a child's education is the enduring goal of #Satchat. All willing and able educators who see what is possible for their students are welcomed to join.
- LinkedIn (www.linkedin.com): Professional networking site that allows educators to connect, exchange ideas, and find opportunities. Educators can join a variety of groups that cater to their individual learning interests and engage in discussions as well as submit, read, and comment on articles.
- Blogs: Incredible sources of information that allow educators to reflect, share opinions, and discuss various topics. This is a common medium with which to discover best practices, examples of innovation, and professional experiences of both novice and veteran educators. Common blogging applications include Blogger (www.blogger.com), Wordpress (wordpress .org), and TypePad (www.typepad.com). Connected

Principals (connectedprincipals.com) is a great example of a collaborative school leader blog that consistently generates great ideas and strategies that can be assimilated into professional practice.

- RSS Readers: RSS stands for "Real Simple Syndication." An RSS reader is a tool that allows leaders to keep up with educational blogs, news, wikis, and podcasts all in one convenient location. By subscribing to various RSS feeds, leaders create a customized flow of information that is continually updated and accessible through the use of mobile devices or the Internet. Leaders can even create their own RSS feeds! Popular RSS readers include Feedly (www.feedly.com) and RSSOwl (www.rssowl.org).

- Tablet and Smartphone Apps: Free apps for iOS (Apple) and Android devices tap into existing RSS feeds and social networks to create customized sources of educational information. The Flipboard app (flipboard.com) will tune any leader's social networks and Feedly RSS feeds into a digital magazine that can be navigated with the flip of a finger. The Zite app (www.zite.com) allows leaders to establish their own categories, and then the app does all of the work. It aggregates all relevant news, blog posts, and video feeds into each customized category, providing digital leaders with only the information that they find most valuable to their growth and development.

- Wikis: Collaborative websites that allow registered users the ability to create and edit any number of interlinked Web pages. Wikis encourage information sharing and collaborative learning. Leaders can view and join some exemplary wiki models at Educational Wikis (educationalwikis.wikispaces.com) and Wikis in Education (wikisineducation.wetpaint.com).

- Digital Discussion Forums: Communities of educators interested in similar topics. One of the most popular sites is called Ning, where educators can create or join specific communities. Ning sites offer a range of learning and growth options such as discussion forums, event postings, messaging, news articles, chat features, groups, and videos. Popular educational Ning sites for leaders include The Educator's PLN (edupln.ning.com), Classroom 2.0 (www.classroom20.com), Administrator 2.0 (admin20.0rg), and School Leadership 2.0 (www.schoolleadership20.com). Some other fantastic digital discussion forums are ASCD Edge (ascdedge.ascd.org), for which you must be a member of ASCD, and edWeb .net. In addition to numerous communities that leaders can tap into, there is one specific to those interested in the principles of digital leadership (www.edweb.net/leadership).

- Social Bookmarking: A method for storing, organizing, curating, and sharing bookmarks online. There are no better tools out there than social bookmarking tools, which allow busy leaders to make order out of the chaos that initially emerges with access to the amazing resources made available through PLNs. Social bookmarking tools allow leaders to store all of their resources in the cloud, which are then accessible from an Internet-connected device. Popular sites such as Delicious (www.delicious.com) and Diigo (www.diigo.com) allow leaders to add descriptions as well as categorize each site using tags. Leaders can even join groups and receive e-mail updates when new bookmarks are added. Diigo has expanded features that allow users to highlight and annotate the websites that they bookmark.
- Facebook: A social networking site that not only allows people to keep up with family and friends, but also to connect and engage with professionals. Many national and state educational organizations have created Facebook pages as places for leaders to congregate online, engage in conversations on professional practice, and share resources. Each customizable page or

group provides a variety of learning opportunities and growth options for educators. Some examples include the National Association of Secondary School Principals (www.facebook.com/principals), National Association of Elementary School Principals (www.facebook .com/naesp), and American Association of School Administrators (www.facebook.com/AASApage).

- Google+: The search giant is at it again with its version of a social networking tool, which contains both Facebook- and Twitter-like attributes. Within Google+, users can create a profile page similar to Facebook, group people in circles (organize people into categories), and set free group video chats called hangouts. Each hangout can include up to ten different people from anywhere in the world.

- Pinterest (pinterest.com): The best way to describe this tool is as an electronic bulletin board where users can "pin" images from around the Web. For visual learners, it is a great way to curate resources and other information. Images that are pinned are categorized into various user-defined boards on one's profile. Images are linked to websites, and pins can be shared and searched for.

Beginning the process of creating and maintaining a PLN can be confusing and at times frustrating. To aid in this transition, leaders can visit a specially designed Google Site that will walk them through the process while providing detailed notes, video tutorials, downloadable documents, and examples of tools mentioned above in practice (sites.google.com/site/anytimepd).

edWeb.net

One of the best learning resources for school leaders is edWeb.net. This previously mentioned digital discussion forum is a professional social and learning network that helps educators connect with colleagues, share expertise and resources, join PLCs, and host individual online communities—all for free. edWeb has grown to nearly 65,000 educators who are at the forefront of innovative ideas and especially forward thinking about integrating technology into teaching and learning. Members are from all over the world, and all levels of education, but conversations and programs are mainly focused on K–12 education.

edWeb hosts online PLCs—with free webinars—that have created a new model for personalized professional learning. edWeb PLCs make it easy for any educator to join a community, watch live or previously recorded webinars, and earn CE certificates for participation. All resources are archived on edWeb, creating an open and free resource for any educator. edWeb won the 2012 Edublog Award for Best Free and Open Professional Development for Educators.

As an educator or school leader, edWeb is a great professional development resource for your teachers, school librarians, and staff. Many schools and districts are embedding edWeb in their professional development programs. You can also use edWeb to create your own PLCs—at no cost. Your communities can be public or private, so they are ideal for professional collaboration. And edWeb provides personal support for members. Help is just an e-mail or phone call away, which is so important for helping educators to learn how to use the latest collaborative technologies. Leaders can join the digital leadership community at www.edweb.net/leadership, which I host. This PLC helps school leaders use Web-based tools to be innovative, help teachers grow professionally, enhance student learning, and improve communications with all stakeholders.

THE PROFESSIONAL GROWTH PERIOD

The Professional Growth Period (PGP) is a job-embedded growth model created at New Milford High School. It arose out of the need for teachers to be able to follow their learning passions as well as form their own PLNs with support from colleagues and administrators. In order to establish the PGP, administrators at New Milford High School had to look at areas of opportunity to free teachers from the current eight-period schedule. The solution came in the form of the noninstructional duties that each teacher was assigned as per the contract—one duty period per day. To make the PGP a reality, all noninstructional teacher duties were cut in half, thus freeing each teacher for two or three 48-minute periods per week, depending on the semester. This resulted in giving my staff the time and flexibility to learn how to integrate the tools that they were interested in, as well as to form their own PLNs.

The key to this model is the autonomy granted teachers to learn about anything that motivates or interests them as long as it has the potential to impact student learning. PGP time is dedicated to engaging in professional learning opportunities in order to become a better educator and learner. Teachers are empowered to follow their passions and work to define a purpose. Teachers are expected to spend this time learning, innovating, and pursuing ways to become master educators. Think of it as a differentiated and personalized learning opportunity that caters to each teacher's specific needs and interests.

In order to give teachers the autonomy that they deserve, each staff member is expected to submit a learning portfolio at their end-of-year evaluation conference. This learning portfolio must demonstrate how PGP time was used to improve professional practice, enhance learning, and ultimately increase student achievement. The learning portfolio becomes a showcase of innovative practices and makes the entire PGP model transparent.

SUMMARY

At the heart of digital leadership is a connected model of learning and professional growth. Connectedness becomes the standard, not just an option or a blatantly discredited method of professional development. Leaders in a digital world embrace and leverage social media to learn any time, from anywhere, and with anyone who might help them do what they do better. The PLNs that they form become invaluable tools that are always at their disposal to help them acquire knowledge, resources, ideas, strategies, advice, and feedback as well as to learn from world-renowned experts and practitioners in the field of education. You don't have to have a PLN to be a great leader, but why would you close the door on the chance to be even better? Learning becomes much more relevant and meaningful as the leader calls the shots and becomes the center of the process. With the empowerment of digital leadership, leaders no longer *attempt* to find the time to learn and get better, but *make* the time to learn and get better.

Source: Couros, A. (2006). Used with permission.

9

Increasing Student Engagement and Enhancing Learning

"A simple question to ask is, 'How has the world of a child changed in the last 150 years?' And the answer is, 'It's hard to imagine any way in which it hasn't changed! But if you look at school today versus 100 years ago, it is more similar than dissimilar.'"

—Peter Senge, senior lecturer,
Massachusetts Institute of Technology

SCHOOL SHOULD REFLECT REAL LIFE

Many of us firmly believe in technology's potential to transform the teaching and learning cultures of schools. Whether it is used to enhance lessons, assess learning, engage students,

133

or unleash creativity, technology has a defined role in a variety of school functions. Even though I am preaching to the choir, many schools still treat education as an effort to prepare students for a world that no longer exists, one in which technology is viewed as either a frill, a distraction, or a nonfactor in improving student achievement.

For many students, school does not reflect real life. This results in various levels of disengagement during the teaching and learning process. The question then becomes, How do we move those schools that are the most irrelevant in terms of meeting the diverse learning needs of their students to begin the transformation process? This is pivotal if we are truly to begin to reform education in a way that is meaningful to our students. Our students want to be creative, collaborate, utilize technology for learning, connect with their peers in other countries, understand the messages that media convey, and solve real-world problems. Schools and systems of education that do not embrace digital learning and place a high emphasis on standardization will always fail to resonate with our students. It only makes sense to harness the power of technology as a catalyst for authentic engagement and application of concepts among our learners. If schools allow students to use the digital-age tools that they are using on a routine basis outside their walls, chances are they will find more relevancy and meaning in what they are learning.

Digital leadership is a mindset and a call to transform a school's culture into one that unleashes the creativity of students so they can create artifacts of learning that demonstrate conceptual mastery. It is about providing learners with the knowledge, skills, and confidence to succeed in college, careers, and jobs that have not even been created yet. Most important, it embraces the concept of Education 3.0, a constructivist, heutagogical approach to teaching and learning. The teachers, learners, networks, connections, media, resources, and tools create a unique entity that has the potential to meet individual learners', educators', and even societal needs (Gerstein, 2013). Digital tools allow for the coconstruction of knowledge, the sharing of experiences, the reflection on practice, the seeking of feedback, and the contribution to the learning of others (Killion, 2013).

This is accomplished by allowing students to use real-world tools to apply what they have learned and construct new knowledge. By focusing on how specific technologies can be used to engage students, digital leaders are establishing a foundation for learning that will lead to eventual increases in student achievement. This becomes a reality when school cultures are transformed to meet and anticipate the needs of learners in the digital age.

It is crucial that sound pedagogical techniques and best practices are emphasized in order to effectively integrate technology to enhance teaching and learning. One of the most important questions a leader needs to answer is how the students are using technology to apply learning and demonstrate conceptual mastery. Students must always be at the center of this process. All too often, technology is infused into the learning environment where the teacher is still employing a direct approach to instruction.

A PEDAGOGICAL FRAMEWORK FOR DIGITAL TOOLS

As a consequence of society's digitization, it becomes increasingly important to use technology in primary as well as in secondary education. Students must achieve a number of digital literacies and competences that will enable them to succeed in a world where digital tools are a natural part of everyday life. To ensure that students acquire the necessary digital literacies and competences and that they can critically think, it is important that they are presented with a range of digital tools and gain an understanding of those tools' capabilities.

This places high demands on the teachers as well as the leaders who support them. It can be difficult to keep up with the new digital opportunities, and it can be hard to assess which digital tools students should be presented with and for which educational contexts they are appropriate. The pedagogical framework of eDidaktik.dk can be the basis for an assessment of whether a digital tool is suitable for use in different forms of teaching.

The framework is based on a distinction between a *monological*, a *dialogical*, and a *polyphonic* form of teaching. The three forms of teaching can be distinguished by their different perceptions of how learning takes place, and by their different perceptions of the relations between subject matter, teacher, and student. By considering which form of teaching one wants to practice, one may, on the basis of the pedagogical framework, assess whether it would be appropriate to use a specific tool in teaching.

The theoretical backgrounds of the monological, the dialogical, and the polyphonic forms of teaching are presented here, and they show how the relations between subject matter, teacher, and student vary in each of the three forms.

The monological form of teaching is based on L. Wittgenstein's idea that the teacher is the expert within a language game and that teaching is to be seen as the teacher's communication of expert knowledge to the student. Learning is the student's acquisition of this knowledge. Prior to the classroom teaching, the teacher defines clear learning objectives and chooses the subject matter that is to be worked with in the classroom. The subject matter is selected so that it distributes the quantity of information that the teacher believes is relevant to the student in relation to the given topic. Along with the teacher's instruction of the student, the subject matter's distribution of information is to ensure that the student learns what the teacher has planned (see Figure 9.1).

After teaching, the teacher will be able to compare the student's learning outcomes with the learning objectives that the teacher defined before the teaching begun. Distributing and integrating tools are particularly relevant within the monological form of teaching, where the transfer of information to the student is a key element. In connection with the evaluation of

Figure 9.1   Monological Teaching

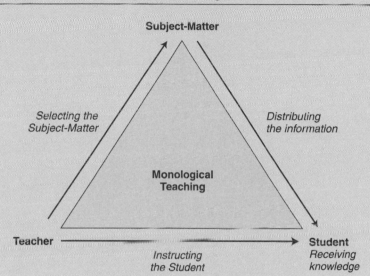

Subject-Matter

Selecting the
Subject-Matter

Distributing
the information

**Monological
Teaching**

Teacher

Instructing
the Student

Student
Receiving
knowledge

Source: Niels (2012). Used with permission.

student learning outcomes, closed tasks and tests are also relevant in this form of teaching.

The dialogical form of teaching is based on J. Dewey's idea that the student has an inherent basis of knowledge that can be developed through interaction with the outside world and by solving problems. Learning is seen as the student's development of this inherent basis of knowledge. The teacher chooses a subject matter, which could make it possible for the student to experience what is relevant and to define and solve authentic problems. In the learning situation, the student chooses to work with the parts of the subject matter that he or she finds relevant and then uses this part of the subject matter as a basis for solving the problem. If there is not enough help inherent in the subject matter in order to solve the problem, the student makes contact with the teacher, who will then act as a supervisor (see Figure 9.2).

Figure 9.2   Dialogical Teaching

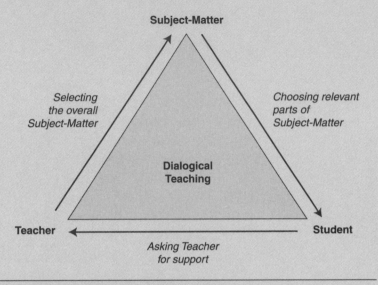

Source: Niels (2012). Used with permission.

The student's learning outcome from dialogic teaching can be tested through case assignments and simulations, where the student can show that he or she can use gained experience within different contexts. Tools that support students' problem-oriented work are especially relevant within the dialogical form of teaching, where the student's gaining of experience is the key element. Simulations and more advanced learning games can also be relevant in this form of teaching.

The polyphonic form of teaching is based on K. E. Løgstrup's idea that knowledge is created through an equal exchange of many different individuals' perceptions of the world. Learning is the student's participation in this exchange. The teacher and student jointly select the subject matter that is to be worked with in the classroom. They are equal in this process, just as they are in their subsequent efforts to process the subject matter and produce common knowledge within the field (see Figure 9.3).

Figure 9.3   Polyphonic Teaching

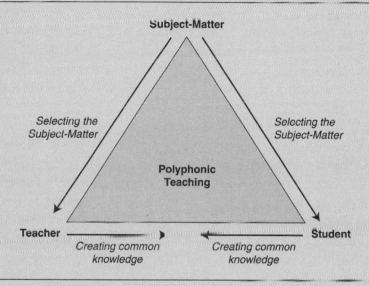

Source: Niels (2012). Used with permission.

The learning outcome cannot easily be measured within a polyphonic form of teaching, but others can subsequently test the validity of the knowledge created in the community of practice, which contributes to the accumulated knowledge within the field. Tools that support equal collaboration and the production of common knowledge are especially relevant within the polyphonic form of teaching, where the equal collaboration on production of knowledge is a key element.

Source: Edudemic. (2012). Pedagogical framework for digital tools. Retrieved from http://edudemic.com/2012/12/a-pedagogical-framework-for-digital-tools/ on March 23, 2013. Adapted with permission.

TWENTY-FIRST-CENTURY LEARNING AT NEW MILFORD HIGH SCHOOL (NJ)

What should learning in schools look like in the twenty-first century? Are schools preparing students for success in a global society? These are two questions that quickly come to mind when reading the quote from Peter Senge. More than ever, it is essential that schools veer away from methodologies that worked for many years when we were educating a different type of student for a different role in society. Key to this transformation is the integration of authentic learning experiences and technology that engage students of all levels and make learning meaningful.

When I came to New Milford High School (NMHS) in 2004, there were many amazing programs in place. One was the Holocaust Study Tour. This global learning endeavor provides some of our students with the opportunity to travel to Europe for at least ten days and study the Holocaust in depth. This authentic learning experience cannot be reproduced in the classroom. For detailed information on the program, please visit The New Milford Holocaust Project (newmilford-holocaustproject.com).

Technology now allows the students and staff at NMHS to share in the authentic learning experiences taking place in Europe (Germany, Poland, Czech Republic). In 2012, we launched a blog where the students in Europe chronicled and reflected on essential questions, focusing on a dark time in human history. Meanwhile, students and staff back on the campus of NMHS have used the blog as a catalyst for a variety of other learning experiences. Some teachers have had their students respond to the posts each day. The Holocaust Study Tour blog can be accessed at hst10.blogspot.com.

Skype has also brought a whole new element to the program. Prior to each trip, students Skype numerous times with their guide, who resides in Israel. Throughout the year, students also Skype with Holocaust survivors in our elective course on the topic. As a leader, I use Skype to keep in contact with my teacher while on the trip and sometimes to converse with the students about what they are learning. We also encourage our history teachers to Skype with the study tour if the times can be worked out. At our District Open House in 2011, we Skyped with the group in Europe to kick off the event. The theme for the event was appropriately centered on what it is like to be a student in the twenty-first century.

A GLOBAL CONTEXT

It is an exciting time to be in education. Technology has really added a whole new dimension to learning in this program as well as many others. Schools that confine themselves to a bland curriculum, textbooks, worksheets, or learning activities that do not go beyond the walls of the brick-and-mortar building are really doing a disservice to their learners. In a society that is now globally connected through easy-to-use and cost-effective Web 2.0 tools, opportunities to engage and make the process of learning meaningful to all students have greatly increased. Teachers now have many tools at their fingertips to add a global context to any lesson.

For example, Skype in the Classroom is a free community that assists teachers in establishing connections between teachers in different countries to help their students learn. Unfortunately, many schools across the country block blogging tools and Skype, as well as a variety of other Web 2.0 technologies that foster creativity, collaboration, problem-solving, and communication skills. As Peter Senge (Newcomb, 2003) alluded, schools have not evolved in step with societal changes. In order to best prepare our students, we must move away from an industrial model of instruction and let go of control in order to meet the diverse needs of today's learners. This will only happen when schools realize that technology is not the enemy. When passionate teachers and visionary schools combine, the end result for students is learning like never before.

Twitter Hash Tags in the Classroom

Students are becoming more and more connected in our world, while classrooms often stay the same. Many educators are starting to embrace connectivity not only for the "social" aspect, but also for the extraordinary learning that can happen. Through the effective use of media like Twitter, some educators are connecting to other incredibly passionate and intelligent educators. To show this power of connected learning in the classroom, many teachers at the junior and high school levels are using hash tags to connect students to one another in the classrooms as well as to the world.

George Couros, the division principal of innovative teaching and learning for the Parkland School Division in Stony Plain, Alberta, Canada, offers the following advice if you are interested in doing something like this with your students. Here are the ways that you can start to set this up for your classroom and students to increase engagement and enhance learning:

- **Think of something easy and as short as possible.** For example, in George's PSD70 Learning Leader Project, he used the hash tag #psd70LLP. This was just an addition of three initials to their school division hash tag to differentiate it from the regular #Psd70 hash tag, making it simple and easy to remember. This advice can be applied to any classroom or school project.
- **Do a search of the hash tag that you want to use**. This is really important, as you want to establish a presence using this hash tag and not be mixed up with another group that is using the same thing. For example, many people use the #AbEd hash tag for Alberta Education, but there is also a small group of people that use #Abed for the character Abed in the show *Community*. There is such a small group of people that use this hash tag that it is barely noticed, but you do not want to be in the minority if you are using this for a class.
- **Figure out a hash tag that can be used for the same subject area across your school.** If you are going to use a hash tag for something like Grade 10 Chemistry, create it with all of the teachers in your school that teach that same subject. This knocks down the physical walls as well as time barriers between classes. You can easily

share the learning from the same course that is delivered at a different time using this hash tag. Once it is figured out, share it with the school, teachers, and parents.

As this type of work has increased in more schools and classrooms, there have been some huge benefits in the form of engagement and meaningful learning from students. For example, George explains that using a hash tag helps to create community learning. If there is an identified hash tag for a course, when you have any lectures (they still have some use in the classroom), students can write their notes publicly and share their learning with one another and be more active participants in their learning. This way, students not only share big ideas during the class, but they can also ask one another questions and be more active participants in that process. It is much more powerful when we are able to connect our learning. Teachers (and students) can also go back and look at the hash tag and see if students understood the concepts or ideas being shared. This helps them to assess their own teaching practice. Not only that, if you are using this between several teachers for a course, it can really emphasize those ideas between courses. This is of great benefit to both teachers and students.

In George's mind, hash tags can help tap into the wisdom of your entire class. Many teachers have their students e-mail them if they are struggling with questions, and the teacher may be able to answer them, but this learning is private and may not address the same question asked from a different student. If you encourage students to use a hash tag to help, then any help can be shared publicly and perhaps address the learning of several people at a time. Not only that. The teacher might not be the one actually answering the question. This is a great way for students to share their learning with one another and see one another as valuable resources in the course. We are much better off and will actually spend less time if we tap into the wisdom of our students.

George identifies that hash tags allow you to share learning with your community. One of the biggest factors in student success is whether or not parents reinforce the learning that is happening in school. This also can start some great conversations at home. We can jump over the question, "What did you learn today?" and actually can get into some deeper conversations about the course that benefit both the learning of the student and the parent. For example, if a parent also follows the hash tag, he or she may say, "I saw that you were learning about _____; tell me more about it." That request totally changes the conversation and the answer.

You are never limited to the learning of your classroom. Even if it is mainly students and teacher(s) following the hash tag, since Twitter is public, George points out that you never know who may jump in on the conversation. If this process becomes the norm, you may have former students helping current students in the program. You may also get questions from students that could be better answered by another educator in such a global network. What I have learned is that there are many passionate educators out there who will help any student, not just those they teach directly.

You are helping kids create a positive digital footprint while also showing how social media can be used for learning. George has asked many students if they see Twitter or Facebook as a tool for learning, and they see no connection. Educators have made good use of Twitter as a professional development tool, and we have to learn how to leverage this in our classroom with students. The other "benefit" of using this with students is that they are building a positive digital footprint and presenting themselves as learners. George would have had no idea how to use Twitter for learning until someone sat down and showed him; educators should start doing the same for our students (Couros, 2013).

A Focus on Essential Skill Sets

The examples provided focus on developing and enhancing essential skill sets that students need to succeed in today's world.

Many know these as twenty-first-century skills, but the conversation must shift as we are now well into the twenty-first century. *Essential skills* is a more applicable term to use for now and the future, as these will always be the cornerstones of student success. To succeed in the new global economy, students need to be able to think like entrepreneurs and be resourceful, flexible, creative, and think globally (Zhao, 2012). This is what employers are desperately looking for in new employees. Essential skills also pave the way for our learners to be prepared to succeed in jobs that have not even been created yet. The only way schools can place learners into positions to seize opportunities present now and in the future is to authentically engage them in learning experiences that are relevant, meaningful, and allow them to apply what has been learned through a variety of means, including the use of digital tools. Essential skills, aligned with both the Common Core Standards and the International Society for Technology in Education's (ISTE) National Educational Technology Standards (NETS) for students and teachers (www.iste.org/standards) include the following:

- **Creativity**—Web 2.0 tools, social media, and mobile learning devices have the power to unleash the creativity of our students. Adobe also is a worldwide leader in providing a host of tools that can unleash creativity of our students. They not only allow students to demonstrate conceptual mastery through learning artifacts, but also allow them to create their own form of art described by Seth Godin (2010). By doing so, a culture of learning is established that will make our students indispensable as they move onward into college and careers.
- **Collaboration**—Digital tools allow students to collaborate on projects and other activities regardless of time and location. This skill provides a competitive advantage to students, as they no longer have to rely on strictly meeting face to face to complete learning tasks together. More and more career paths rely on teamwork to complete projects through the use of technology.

- **Communication**—Effective communication is one of the most important skills needed to succeed in today's society. Digital tools expose students to a variety of means to communicate in the real world through social networks, Web 2.0 tools, and video conferencing.
- **Critical Thinking and Problem Solving**—Digital tools provide learners with the media to reason effectively through both induction and deduction; use systems thinking; solve problems in innovative ways; and make judgments and decisions through analysis, reflection, synthesis, and evaluation. They can also be used to solve complete problems and develop unique solutions that traditional means cannot.
- **Entrepreneurism**—An often overlooked or under-valued skill, entrepreneurism can be developed and enhanced through the use of digital tools to solve problems and create artifacts of learning. It instills a sense of taking risks and dealing with failure along the road to success when constructing new knowledge and applying skills to demonstrate learning. Allowing students to create apps, games, websites, business plans, virtual worlds, and videos can play a role in developing and enhancing this skill.
- **Global Awareness**—Web-based tools and other forms of technology empower students to connect with peers across the globe and develop a better understanding of issues, customs, cultures, architecture, and economics. In a globally connected world, this skill has become sought after by employers whose professions know no geographical bounds.
- **Technological Proficiency**—The importance of this skill goes without saying. The more reliant society becomes on technology, the more we must effectively embed it into the teaching and learning culture to adequately prepare students for the real world.
- **Digital Media Literacy**—Students today need to be given opportunities to create and consume digital

content in order to develop essential literacies. They need to learn how to interpret an array of new messages conveyed through digital media. Appendix E provides some excellent ideas on how digital tools can be used to foster this essential skill while engaging learners in an authentic fashion during the instructional process.

- **Digital Responsibility, Citizenship, and Footprints—** When schools routinely integrate technology for learning, they in turn teach their students how to use it appropriately. They also empower students to develop positive digital footprints when they create content online or share it through social media. These experiences then develop skills that students can and will use to their advantage well beyond their school years

The integration of Web-based resources, skills, and technology allows students to use real-world tools to solve real-world problems. Digital leadership places a strategic focus on developing a teaching and learning culture that is not only student centered, but also empowers learners to construct their own meanings and essential understandings of concepts by nontraditional means. It is ever so important to make sure learning outcomes are associated with the use of these tools. The following image (Figure 9.4) created by Bill Ferriter (2013) hammers home this point.

This type of learning can be, and most often is, messy at first, as this shift requires school leaders to give up control. In addition to giving up a certain level of control, leaders must grant teachers autonomy to take calculated risks in order to discover ways to develop innovative practices that combine digital tools with sound pedagogy. This shift leading to change and eventual transformation is a difficult process.

THE MOVE TO 1:1

When looking around Burlington School District in Burlington, Massachusetts, it is hard for Patrick Larkin, the

Figure 9.4   Using Technology as a Tool to Facilitate Deeper
Learning

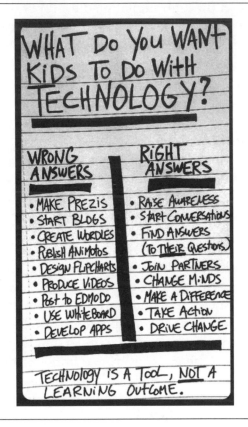

Source: Ferriter (2013). Used with permission.

assistant superintendent for learning, to believe how quickly they have made the transition from a district that banned devices in classrooms to one that went out and purchased over 2,000 mobile devices so that staff and students could have access to more educational resources throughout the school day. They used to deny the changes that were happening outside of their school doors because they could not deal with what they thought might happen if they were to allow students to have the Internet at their fingertips while sitting in classrooms. However, when they made an honest assessment of their mission statement that charged them with preparing all students for the "real world" and coupled that with the amazing things happening with technology in the real world outside of their doors, Patrick and other administrators knew it was time to take off their blinders and make some changes.

In reality, the thing that was holding them back was their own past experiences. Yes, the adults in the school were handicapped by their own pasts. As students, they experienced little to no technology in the classroom and a great degree of micromanagement for each move they made. In turn, they were prepared to pass on this same degree of rigidity to their own students. There was also the lack of trust shown by administrators who would not allow staff to utilize mobile devices, even when they had concrete educational tasks tied to their lessons.

However, somewhere along the line, something changed for them. The starting point may have been when they looked at some data that told them that, despite the fact that they did not allow mobile devices in school, more than 95% of their students were sending and receiving multiple text messages each day. Or maybe it was when they began to look more closely at the district's mission statement, which contained phrases like *lifelong learning* and *responsible citizenship*, and came to the realization that they could not do either to the fullest extent if they had the most modern learning resources on lockdown.

After a great deal of discussion among staff members, Burlington High School, under the leadership of then-principal Patrick Larkin, decided to take a small step outside of their comfort zone and modify the existing policy regarding the use of digital devices in school. For the 2009–2010 school year, they made a change to their policy and allowed mobile devices to be utilized in the classroom "at the teacher's discretion." Ultimately, it was agreed that staff and students needed more access to resources in their classrooms, not less.

Amazingly enough, a year later, the leaders were so comfortable with the decision that they formed a planning team to devise a way to get a device in the hands of every student throughout the school day and become a 1:1 school. Teachers realized that putting devices in the hands of all students opened up more possibilities than problems, and they were on their way. The school administrative team encouraged staff members to try new things and share successes, and not to worry about failures. At the same time, a new classroom walk-through protocol called "learning walks" initiated conversations about classroom engagement and increased discussions about effective strategies and resources that could help create higher levels of student engagement.

Speaking of student engagement, one of the most important aspects of their 1:1 planning team was the inclusion of students as equal members at the table helping to chart the path. After a bit of discussion with students about this initiative, it became clear that they were not just typical members of the planning team. Their thoughtful insights and suggestions made it clear early on that they were equal partners in this endeavor who would need to have significant roles in this change in order to be successful. This gave rise to the idea of the BHS Student Help Desk, a semester course for students who were interested in technology and/or problem solving.

While Patrick and other Burlington leaders knew that the Student Help Desk was a good idea, they never imagined how successful it would become. Administratively, the idea was partially due to the fact that the district IT staff, comprised of three individuals, could never handle all of the issues that the addition of 1,000 new iPad devices would bring. They wanted to ensure that when there were questions or problems with the devices, staff and students could get a quick response. Not only did students handle each question that came their way, they also started a blog on which they posted information on the iOS updates and video tutorials for various digital resources and apps.

On top of the day-to-day support of Burlington staff and students, the students have spoken to hundreds of visiting educators who have come through the school looking to implement similar programs. They have also spoken at local and regional conferences about their experiences, providing honest answers and advice to educators from all over New England, just as they did for us at the start of the journey (Larkin, 2013).

While the basic goal at the start of this initiative was to bring more resources into the school by providing teachers and students access to digital tools, something much more significant has taken place. There has been clear movement made away from teacher-led learning environments and a transition to learner-led environments where teachers and students are learning together. By including the voices of students in this undertaking, worlds have collided, and a very interesting phenomenon has taken place: Technology-experienced students have joined forces with pedagogically experienced educators to bring about some amazing changes.

The truth of the matter is that it has nothing to do with devices and has everything to do with rethinking what our students need to prepare them for the rapidly changing real world beyond the school walls.

BYOD: An Idea Whose Time Has Come

As we continue to move even further into the century, technology becomes more embedded in all aspects of society. I see this firsthand with my son, who is in second grade. The gift he wanted the most this past Christmas was an iPod Touch, which Santa was kind enough to bring him. Then there is his younger sister, who will regularly ask to use my iPad so she can either care for her virtual horse or dress Barbies in creative ways. As I download all of the apps on these devices, the majority of their time is spent engaged in games that require thought, creativity, and sometimes collaboration. My point here is that many children across the world have access to and are using technology outside of school in a variety of ways. Not only do many have access, but also older children possess their own devices—that is, cell phones, smartphones, laptops, tablets, e-readers, etc.

As society continues to move forward in terms of innovation, technology, and global connectivity, schools have been stymied by relentless cuts to education. This has resulted in the reduction of staff, larger class sizes, lack of follow-through to repair aging buildings, and the inability to keep up with purchasing and replacing educational technology. It is essential that we rectify all of the above-mentioned impacts of budget cuts, but when it comes to technology, the perception is that it is the least important element for those precious funds. This is why the time is now for districts and schools to seriously consider developing a Bring Your Own Device (BYOD) initiative to further engage students in the teaching and learning process in a cost-effective fashion.

The world of education is often defined by the "haves" and "have-nots." It is this separation that ultimately drives decisions when it comes to educational technology. Why should students in less affluent districts not be afforded the same opportunity as those with large budgets to utilize technology to create, collaborate, connect, communicate, and develop essential media literacies? A BYOD initiative makes sense, as we can now leverage a variety of devices that many of our students already possess. It is how we utilize these student-owned devices in schools that are the key to a successful BYOD initiative.

There are many well-respected educators that I also greatly admire who feel that BYOD has no place in schools. Their main reasons for this are equity in terms of students who do not have devices and the belief that it is each district's responsibility to provide all technology to be used by students in schools. I wholeheartedly agree with their positions, but those of us in the trenches must play with the cards that we have been dealt. As educators, it is our duty to do everything in our power to provide our students with the best learning opportunities possible. In many cases, allowing students to bring their own devices to school assists in meeting this lofty goal.

We launched our BYOD program at New Milford High School in September of 2011. There have been many lessons learned from this journey, the most important being that the students have greatly appreciated this shift. Policies have been developed for students to bring in their own computing devices; a ban on cell phone use during noninstructional times has been lifted; and educational programs have been put in place to teach our students about digital citizenship, responsibility, and digital footprints. We did not let excuses like equity issues stop us from moving forward with an initiative that is turning out to have real value to our students and teachers. Key components of a successful BYOD initiative include the following:

- Begin to change the way students view their devices by changing the language used to refer to them. Students need to fully understand that they are tools for learning. Make consistent efforts to refer to them as mobile learning devices.
- Attach a specific learning outcome to devices when using them in the classroom.
- Determine in a confidential manner which students don't own devices and ensure that all have access. For example, if a school has a laptop cart with only twenty devices because that's all the funding provides, but there are twenty-five students in the class, student-owned technology can be shared to close the gap. If the class is using mobile phones, teachers can easily pair students up.
- Develop appropriate support structures that align with current Acceptable Use Policies.
- Provide professional development and resources to teachers so that they can be successful in implementing mobile learning devices.

- Treat students like twenty-first-century adolescents. Many of them own and use these devices outside of school. If we can focus use on learning, then why would we not allow them to bring these tools and use them in school?
- Unacceptable use is dealt with accordingly, based on a school's discipline code. This should not be considered different than any other infraction. When it comes to off-task behavior in the classroom, this is most likely the result of a poorly planned lesson or ineffective classroom management techniques.
- Promote use of student-owned devices for learning during noninstructional time. At NMHS, one can now routinely see students using their devices during lunch to conduct research for projects, complete homework assignments, and organize their responsibilities. Additionally, we have seen a dramatic reduction in behavior issues.

Instead of bashing BYOD and coming up with ideas on how and why it won't work or is unfair, we would best be served to brainstorm ways in which it can become an educational component of our schools. The excuses to write off BYOD only serve to undermine the students we are tasked with educating. A BYOD initiative will be unique to each district and should be carefully constructed based on socioeconomics and community dynamics. To begin the process, students should be asked for their input. Digital leadership looks beyond the excuses for why it can't work and looks toward possible solutions to better engage learners now and in the future.

BLENDED LEARNING

Creating a student-centered learning environment is vital to making the learning process enjoyable, increasing levels of student engagement, improving student retention of the material taught, providing students with the opportunity to develop twenty-first-century skills, and ultimately improving student performance. Through the use of technology, collaborative learning exercises, and teaching mathematical concepts in the real-world and interdisciplinary context, Kanchan Chellani, a New Milford High School mathematics educator, has managed to successfully create this desired positive and energetic blended learning environment.

Kanchan's path to building an innovative classroom began when she started integrating SMART Board interactive content review games and videos at the start of each class in order to reinforce prior learning in an interactive, engaging, and differentiated fashion. Through Internet searches and resource libraries such as YouTube, Kanchan has been able to find valuable games and video content aligned to the content being taught in class. No matter whether or not her students feel confident in their mathematical abilities, she has noticed that they will never hesitate either to come up to the SMART Board to work on a problem or watch an educational video. Infusing interactive content review games and videos at the beginning of each class not only serves as an additional means to formally assess students, but also creates positive energy in the classroom, engages the learner, and allows students to learn the material in a differentiated and interactive fashion . . . some without even realizing it!

In addition to SMART Board interactive content review games and videos, Kanchan wanted to utilize and share the knowledge and skills she had gained during her professional experience as a financial analyst to make the mathematical content more meaningful for her students. As a result, she decided to integrate case studies as a means to reinforce learning. For example, for the case study she had written for the unit on quadratics in her Algebra II class, students were asked to go onto www.finance.yahoo.com, retrieve share prices for Citigroup, Inc. for a specified period of time, use trend and regression analysis to analyze the data on MS Excel, and answer questions on the analysis in order to ensure comprehension of the findings. As illustrated, the case studies have been designed to connect key mathematical concepts to real-life and other disciplines so students are better able to comprehend the content as well as understand its significance. Furthermore, these case studies provide students with the opportunity to enhance their technological skills (i.e., MS Office applications, Internet research, trend/statistical analysis, etc.) as well as foster an environment for students to collaborate and develop higher-order thinking skills that prepare them with essential skill sets.

Although incorporating both interactive review games/ videos and case studies have transformed the learning environment for her students, Kanchan wanted to do more to differentiate her teachings and enhance the learning experience for them. Through discussions with her colleagues, attending the annual Edscape conference held at New Milford High School, and continually brainstorming, she kept finding new and innovative ways that would allow her to create an even stronger, student-centered learning environment. One of the things she infuses at the very start of class is a warm-up question displayed on the SMART Board through Poll Everywhere, a free, online polling tool. With the school's BYOD initiative, students are able to text their answers to the warm-up anonymously, using their own personal cell phone devices. Results are then revealed and discussed prior to beginning the SMART Board interactive review game or video. Additionally, since the "flipped" approach to instruction is proving to be a key asset in modern education, another initiative of hers has been to provide students with a means to learn independently utilizing digital content. She began using Edmodo, an online platform that enables innovative and social learning, as a way to share online videos and content on the relevant topic for her students to view and assign online polls for her students to complete. By assigning these videos as homework, she is able to have students develop a foundational or working knowledge of the relevant mathematical topic that fosters discussion in class and promotes a collaborative working environment. Additionally, it provides ample class time to dive deeper into key mathematical topics and for students to engage in projects, case studies, Web quests, activities, virtual manipulatives, and content review games to reinforce the learning. Although enabling the "flipped" approach to instruction using Edmodo has transformed the way material is taught and comprehended by students, it has been difficult for her to find resources that combine curriculum delivery, real-world examples, and assessments in a cohesive manner. As a result, she started to create her own online learning modules, using the software Adobe Captivate.

Adobe Captivate is a type of digital content creation software that fosters interactive eLearning content. She has made use of the tool by creating learning modules that teach the basic mathematical concepts as well as provide practice problems, real-world examples, and assessments that allow for better comprehension of the material in an organized fashion. In these learning modules, instruction is provided using digital content, simulations, videos, screen captures, voice-overs, etc., to meet the visual, auditory, and tactile needs of the diverse student population. Once the instruction has been provided, guided practice problems and real-world examples are then discussed to reinforce the learning of the mathematical concept and to illustrate its significance. A variety of prompts and formal assessments are also embedded within the project in order to ensure that the learning has taken place, to develop higher-order thinking skills, and to facilitate discussion in the classroom.

Through the integration of warm-ups via Poll Everywhere, the BYOD initiative, SMART Board interactive content review games and videos, case studies, and flipping instruction in a captivating fashion, Kanchan has been able to successfully create an effective, twenty-first-century, student-centered learning environment. As illustrated, her motivation and dedication to enhance the learning experience for her students have provided her with the drive to continually experiment with new and innovative techniques that are engaging, relevant, and meaningful to her students. Furthermore, this environment has provided them with the opportunity to develop the essential skill sets needed to succeed after the secondary education.

DIGITAL CITIZENSHIP

Just because today's students have grown up in a technology-rich world does not mean that they know how to effectively and responsibly utilize technology. It is a common misconception that today's learners can seamlessly transition from the routine use of devices for personal reasons to using them for learning, research, and enhanced productivity. We routinely hear how students use digital tools inappropriately for sexting, cyberbullying, cheating, video-recording teachers and fights with peers, and plagiarizing. Unfortunately, these behaviors have become quite common, as schools are not doing their part to educate students on digital responsibility, citizenship, and creating a positive footprint online.

At New Milford High School, we have made it our responsibility to integrate digital responsibility across the curriculum. Our program begins early in the school year with assemblies for every grade level. During this time, we present the root causes of cyberbullying as well as strategies and advice to prevent it. We then transition into online conduct in social media spaces and how that can impact college acceptances and employment. During this part of the presentation, I point out to students the fact that once they post something online (i.e., comments, pictures, videos, etc.), that information can be accessed, adapted, archived, and shared by anyone who has access to their accounts. Near the end of the presentation, we ask each student to Google themselves and share with us any content they discovered during the search that they were not aware of. It is at this point that reality really sets in.

In addition to a presentation early in the year, we consistently integrate digital tools (social media, Web 2.0, mobile devices) throughout the school year to enhance learning, improve productivity, and conduct sound research. As students actively use these tools to connect, collaborate, contribute, and create, they are developing media literacy skills. Teachers also work with students to properly cite resources pulled from the Web, and to give proper credit when they see it is governed by a Creative Commons license (creativecommons.org). As they publish their own work in the form of learning artifacts, they begin to create a positive digital footprint that they can be proud of. The systematic integration of technology, modeling of effective use by school staff, education programs for both students and parents, and an immersive culture (1:1 or BYOD) all aid in educating students on digital citizenship. Common Sense Media offers a free digital literacy and citizenship curriculum that leaders can easily begin to implement in their schools. This can be accessed at www.commonsensemedia.org/educators/curriculum.

SUMMARY

The most important aspect of digital leadership is establishing a vision and a strategic plan for increasing authentic engagement of students in the teaching and learning process. An emphasis must first be placed on the pedagogy in order to successfully integrate the wealth of Web-based tools that are available for free. When students are allowed to use real-world tools to apply what they have learned to demonstrate conceptual mastery and solve real-world problems, their experiences in school become more relevant and meaningful. Implementing either a 1:1 or a BYOD program not only places digital tools in the hands of students, but also empowers them to further develop essential skill sets, take more control of their learning, and become more responsible in these areas. It is extremely important for leaders to create a culture that not only supports the use of tools for learning, but also teaches students about digital citizenship.

10

Rethinking Learning Environments and Spaces

Gahanna is a middle- to upper-middle-class suburban community with more than 53,000 residents, including a little more than 7,000 students, located outside Columbus, Ohio. There are eleven schools that make up the Gahanna Jefferson Public School District: seven elementary schools, three middle schools, and one high school. Gahanna Lincoln High School (GLHS) is a sprawling building that gained a number of additions over the years to accommodate a growing student body. However, despite attempts to contain student growth within the current structure, the student enrollment continued to climb to more than 2,400 in 2009. An audit by the Ohio School Facilities Commission that year revealed that the high school was over capacity, falling short 71,000 square feet by their code, and unable to accommodate all of their students. The challenge of finding more space for an overcrowded building presented a unique opportunity to do something different than building a second high school. This is where the Clark Hall story begins.

Shift 1—Establishing a Better Vision

Former Gahanna Jefferson Public Schools superintendents Gregg Morris and Mark White had the vision, the financial understanding, and the courage to launch the Clark Hall project as a way to reduce crowding in the current high school building. Instead of asking the community for a second high school—something that the community of Gahanna was adamantly against——they came up with the concept of a creative learning environment with the input from a number of stakeholders. They quickly realized that this could be the opportunity to do something creative to provide more space for students while meeting the needs of today's learner. Together with the vision of Morris and White and the hard work of a team of curriculum coordinators, business directors, and highly qualified teachers, they decided to build Clark Hall. The team included Dwight Carter, the building principal who fully understands and operates by the Pillars of Digital Leadership.

Shift 2—Strengthening and Opening Up the Wireless Network

To prepare for their transformative building, coined "the spearhead of change" by Dell Education Consultant Mark Weston, they first had to address problems with their current network. The type or number of devices is insignificant if the wireless network is unable to handle the digital, technological, and creative needs of today's students and teachers. While they were a wireless campus, they experienced significant problems on a nearly daily basis. This problem was compounded when the decision was made to open the campus to allow students to use their own mobile devices, creating a BYOD environment.

As the year progressed, there were many problems with the existing network. It was not only slow, but many of the sites students wanted to access were blocked. Laptops were especially slow. It got to the point where teachers would rather plan lessons without technology than deal with the issues they were running into daily. The complaint was constant: "It takes the students forever to log on!" Dwight and other administrators went around placing blame on the technology team, the "old computers," and whatever else they could think of. It wasn't until much later, however, that Dwight realized it was his own fault! He didn't talk with the technology coordinator about opening up his campus to mobile devices prior to doing so, and the increase of use had quickly clogged the network.

While this was a major problem, it forced them to focus on the fact that before any more devices could be added—school purchased or BYOD—they had to upgrade the existing wireless network. Morris and White, with the assistance of Technology Coordinator Joe Schiska, negotiated a deal with Cisco Systems to drive down the pricing to upgrade their wireless network across the district. This was the most important component of the technology integration plan. In the words of Joe Schiska, "We went from a two-lane highway to a two-thousand-lane highway" in terms of the speed and accessibility of the network. With this hurdle out of the way, the Gahanna team began to prepare teachers for what it would mean to teach and learn in such a unique environment.

SHIFT 3—A CHOICE TO TEACH AND LEARN A DIFFERENT WAY

Teachers assigned to Clark Hall, year one, were placed there on their own accord. All teachers were told that, while the focus would be on student learning, a large expectation for technology use and integration would be placed upon their lessons. Thus, in preparation for Clark Hall, this addition to the campus, about forty teachers and administrators (thirty-five GLHS staff and five district staff) participated in a three-day social media/Web 2.0 tools boot camp called Kip Camp on The Ohio State University campus. It was at Kip Camp that Dwight learned how other educators were using social media and Web tools like Diigo, Edmodo, Schoology, Twitter, and Google Search to engage learners.

As additional preparation for teaching in such a different environment, the Gahanna team did a book study with teachers and administrators using Ian Jukes's book, *Teaching Today's Digital Generation: No More Cookie Cutter High Schools.* This stretched their thinking and provided a framework for them to move forward. Through this study, they focused on

- Time Management: How are we going to help students manage their time to optimize learning?
- Collaboration: How are we going to provide opportunities for students to collaborate with one another to solve problems and create content?
- Technology Integration: How are we going to get the technology into the hands of the students so they own their learning?
- Content Delivery: How can we transition from a teacher-centered classroom to a student-centered learning environment?

As a culmination of this book study, Ian Jukes visited the district and shared his knowledge of twenty-first-century learning with the staff. Much of his focus centered on technology, not just for the sake of having technology, but technology in the hands of students on a daily basis to be used as a tool for learning. With this concept in mind, Dwight then sent four of the teachers who wanted to teach at Clark Hall to a project-based learning (PBL) conference with the understanding that it would be their responsibility to share their learning with others upon return. PBL was chosen because the principles of PBL complemented the established objectives, including the importance of technology integration and student voice/choice (Carter, 2013).

Shift 4—A New Building Construct

After two years of planning, Clark Hall opened at the start of the 2010–2011 academic year. Clark Hall is a 51,000 square foot, three-story work of art. It doesn't resemble a typical American high school at all, but rather an innovative office building. The objectives of Clark Hall are to

- Provide an open, bright, and flexible space for learning
- Provide student choice
- Integrate technology to engage students
- Be flexible with time to focus on learning
- Provide students with the opportunities to express their natural creativity
- Utilize teachers as facilitators
- Promote interdisciplinary and interconnected projects
- Make learning fun!

With flexibility built into the daily schedule, teachers had more time to interact with students on an individual basis, students felt more relaxed and were more compelled to engage in the learning process, and collaboration among students just seemed natural. The entire building became a learning environment, not just the classrooms. They have soft seating throughout the building: in the two common areas, in seven of the fourteen classrooms, in several small conference rooms, and in the hallways. At any time during the day, visitors will see pockets of students working individually or collaboratively on their laptops completing assignments while the teachers are in the classrooms working with individual students. There are also soft-seating nooks in the hallways that resemble a modern university student commons: Students are lounging on the chairs within the classroom and hallway spaces diligently using their laptops to write blogs, research, complete projects, or complete assignments posted on the teacher portals.

Dwight and the Gahanna team got away from the traditional beige walls and standard furniture because they wanted a space that was comfortable, less formal or institutional, and evoked creativity. They returned to the days of elementary school, where there are bright colors like lime green, bright orange, red, gold, and royal blue. They chose splashes of color on the walls and bright, colorful modular furniture. Half of the classrooms don't have traditional desks or chairs, but instead have couches, soft armless chairs, ottomans on wheels, café-style tables, and exercise balls for students to sit on. There are also brightly colored area rugs in classrooms to soften up the spaces a bit. When students are asked what they think about Clark Hall, their responses are the same: "It's so comfortable over here. I can think and do my work; it feels like I'm in college because I have freedom, but there is also a lot of responsibility to get my work done; I love the bright, open spaces! It's not like main campus; I love all the technology! The laptops work and the wireless is so fast. It makes it a lot easier to use it to complete projects."

Each classroom and small conference room has a short throw LCD projector connected to a desktop computer so lessons can be interactive and students can use them as well. Each room is also wired for surround sound with a microphone to help project the teacher's voice. Dwight has found that lessons are more interactive, engaging, and visual with the effective integration of technology. The modular furniture adds to the flexibility.

Clark Hall has inspired change on Gahanna High School's main campus as well. One of the main hubs of most schools and universities is the library. They wanted their library to have the same feel as Clark Hall, so their librarian, Ann Gleek, dreamed big and made some significant changes: removing some of the book shelves, painting the walls, and changing some of the furniture to reflect the informal style of Clark Hall. These changes have made for a more inviting environment for students and have been a huge hit.

SHIFT 5—CREATING A REAL-WORLD SPACE

Clark Hall houses fourteen classrooms, each with its own conference room attached for small-group work or breakout sessions. In addition, the building contains high-powered wireless Internet connections, natural light, laptops for every student, collaborative spaces in the hallways so students are able to utilize the entire space for learning, and leased spaced on the first floor. The revenue from these leases helps to pay off the mortgage for this property in a shorter amount of time. It was accomplished through the vision of former superintendents Morris and White, along with District Treasurer Julio Valledaras, who worked with legislators to change the laws to allow the district to lease space on the first floor of Clark Hall. Currently, the space is occupied by Eastland Fairfield Career Center and Columbus State Community College. The leases from these two entities will help the district pay off the mortgage. Additionally, a strategic partnership has been formed with a land developer who built 9,000 and 14,000 square foot buildings at the front of the property to lease to retailers. As of December 2012, the retail space is at 100% capacity, with businesses like Panera, Chipotle, AT&T, and the Rusty Bucket serving students and the community at large. The Clark Hall building is now a thriving economic model that benefits the community, the students, and the schools. All of this was accomplished without raising property taxes.

SHIFT 6—STRATEGIC PARTNERSHIPS

Dwight and the Gahanna team also formed a strategic partnership with the YMCA. The YMCA provided more than $55,000 of exercise equipment to outfit one room in Clark Hall and now uses it as an annex to provide evening classes for its members. Some of the high school's physical education classes use it during the day, and it has led to the creation of a fitness club that meets twice a week after school. They had had a partnership with the Eastland-Fairfield Career Center, so Gahanna Lincoln High School was the satellite location for the Architecture Technology program. This program moved to the first floor of Clark Hall with two new programs: Teacher Professions, which prepares students for careers in education, and the Bioscience Technology program, one of the fastest growing fields in the country. These programs are cutting edge and provide relevant opportunities for students. The students in the Architecture program actually helped to design their room and were able to walk through the site as it was being constructed.

Clark Hall has been one of the most exciting additions to the Gahanna District. It has given teachers the freedom to explore and take calculated risks in the classroom, and has provided a unique learning experience for students. It is helping them not only to reform what they do, but transform how they do it. Besides curriculum and assessment, educational reform must include reforming or transforming the physical learning environment. According to Daniel Pink (2011), design is one of the elements of the right brain that we must tap into. We have to look differently at the space we have now and spruce things up . . . a lot . . . for the sake of learning.

DESIGNING SCHOOLS TO ENGAGE AND DRIVE LEARNING

The story of Clark Hall represents a needed shift in school design and a glimpse of how learning environments can be restructured to better meet the diverse and unique needs of today's learners. Digital leadership looks at societal trends as inspirational elements and potential catalysts for change in the structure of the schools themselves as well as the designs of programs. The environment of Google presents many of these elements for leaders to reflect upon when looking to move toward change in this area.

On a recent trip to Google's offices in New York City, I noticed many features that made the office stand out, such as the use of scooters as a means of transportation. There were even racks throughout each floor where Google employees could park their scooters. One could not miss the Lego wall in a lounge area. The wall was lined with bins of different sized and colored Legos. It was clear that employees are encouraged to unleash their creativity when it suits them. Specialized areas and rooms were located throughout the building. These included gaming, nap, and massage rooms, which catered to the diverse interests of Google employees. A great deal of emphasis was placed on food, as there were mini-kitchens galore. It was obvious that appetite content-ment is a priority at Google. Some of these kitchens were decorated in particular themes. One of the most elaborate mini-kitchens was decorated as a jungle, complete with hammock-like chairs, small waterfalls, decorated trees, and live frogs. Equally impressive were the massive espresso, cappuccino, and coffee machines in each kitchen, as well as the overwhelming selection of foods and beverages and a bistro dining area that provides employees with an unparal-leled lunch. Lunch is truly a dining experience, and there is an immense selection of choices.

Google-themed artwork was visible throughout the building. Company pride was apparent everywhere. Clever reminders not to do certain things were located throughout the space. One sign posted throughout the building was a pic-ture of an alligator with its tail propping the door open with this reminder: "Beware the Tailgator!" Obviously, Google doesn't want some doors propped open for security reasons. Office spaces contained entire walls that were transformed into whiteboards, perfect for brainstorming and outlining cre-ative ideas. Many of these offices even had a large table that could seat twelve to sixteen people. Open spaces with com-fortable furniture that invites collaboration (leather couches, plush lounge chairs, etc.), not to mention more coffee stations, were also readily apparent.

The atmosphere described above really inspires and motivates employees to perform at a consistently high level, along with Google's 80/20 Innovation Model, where Google engineers are encouraged to take 20% of their time to work on something company-related that interests them personally (Mediratta, 2007). Who wouldn't want to work in this type of environment? Now, imagine what would happen if schools adopted a similar thought process and designed learning and common spaces using the principles described above? Digital leadership anticipates the potential this could have on increasing achievement, motivation, and developing a passion for the learning process. Such a transition—along with the integration of the other Six Pillars of Digital Leadership—creates schools that students can't wait to get to and are reluctant to leave at the end of the day. School redesign needs to become part of the education reform conversation. Digital leadership makes this a reality.

Academies

In addition to school design, digital leadership anticipates the types of programs needed to authentically engage learners during their school experience while providing environments that focus on college and career readiness in a digital world. Even though the Common Core Standards provide a framework to begin this process, it is incumbent upon leaders to develop holistic programs that allow students to follow their learning passions, engage in a cohort style of learning, and utilize constructivist theory to create their own essential understandings in academic areas.

Academy programs represent a bold new direction for education, one that considers student interests, national need, and global demand for highly qualified graduates capable of competing at the most challenging levels. They provide a defined framework for studies in well-defined, career-focused areas directly connected to university majors and workforce need. These programs cultivate emerging professionals who exhibit the knowledge, skill, character, and work ethic necessary for success in the global marketplace. In September 2011, the Academies@New Milford High School were launched. This initiative was a result of the vision of New Milford School

District Superintendent Michael Polizzi and the strategic planning of Director of Curriculum and Instruction Danielle Shanley. In addition to the array of career-focused curricula associated with each of the Academies, there are special features that further define the Academy experience:

- Professional mentorships
- Opportunities for dual credit
- Access to resources, field trips, and virtual courses outside school settings
- Book studies
- Relationships with partnering institutions and organizations, such as The Bergen Performing Arts Center (BergenPAC), St. Thomas Aquinas College, and Farleigh Dickinson University
- Master classes, workshops, and other related field studies
- A capstone project
- Specialized transcripts
- A special designation on diploma

Michael Polizzi and Danielle Shanley not only anticipated the needs of New Milford students that aligned with societal shifts, but demonstrated bold leadership to develop and successfully launch the Academies. The entire program was designed using existing high school courses as well as adding new ones to complement the three Academies—STEM (Science, Technology, Engineering, and Math), Arts & Letters, and Global Leadership—without costing the district precious financial resources. After the first year, funds were put aside to support extending learning opportunities for Academy students, which mainly consisted of transportation for field trips. The entire philosophy as well as descriptions of the three Academies and endorsements can be accessed at issuu.com/newmilfordschools/docs/academies. By creating our own Academies and integrating them into the current structure, New Milford High School was able to dramatically change how students learn. This program is available to any student who wishes to push himself or herself more, regardless of academic ability, while pursing unique interests.

Individualized and Personalized Learning

Possibly one of the most important shifts needed in schools is to provide individualized and personalized learning experiences to students. Learning has fundamentally changed with the evolution of the Internet and other technologies that allow for ubiquitous access to information and knowledge. Digital leadership focuses on transforming learning environments through online course offerings (synchronous and asynchronous), independent studies, and use of OpenCourseWare to provide students with continuous options to learn any time, anywhere, and about anything.

Infusing online learning opportunities should be a given in a digital world. There is no excuse not to secure funds to better meet the needs of gifted learners or those with specialized interests. States that do not have their own online course consortia can become a member of the VHS Collaborative (thevhscollaborative.org). Either pathway to online courses opens up an existing course catalogue to hundreds of additional niche courses that cater to specific student interests. In the case of the VHS Collaborative, it offers more than 200 courses taught by certified teachers, including virtually every Advanced Placement course accredited by the College Board. High school leaders can make these available to students to take on their own time in addition to the courses they take at their home schools. They can also insert them into their existing class schedules in lieu of electives. Either way, the result is expanded course offerings and learning opportunities for students to personalize and individualize their educational experience.

One of the most cost-effective means to create a more personalized and individualized learning experience for students is through the use of OpenCourseWare (OCW) and Massive

Open Online Course (MOOC). Perhaps one day, the twenty-first century will be remembered as the time when knowledge became available to everyone for free. Pioneers in open learning like Wikipedia have harnessed the collective intellect of the planet "to collect and develop educational content under a free license or in the public domain, and to disseminate it effectively and globally."

Prestigious centers of learning are also making good use of the Internet's power to share knowledge in the form of OCW. OCW can best be defined as high-quality digital publications created by leading American universities that are organized as courses of study, offered free of charge, and delivered via the Internet. OCW courses are available under open licenses, such as Creative Commons. These courses allow for personalization of studies as students explore topics of their choosing.

The Independent OpenCourseWare Study (IOCS) Program developed by Tenafly Middle School teacher Juliana Meehan and me and pioneered at New Milford High School represents a bold, authentic learning experience for secondary students that allows them to fully utilize OCW to pursue learning that focuses on their passions, interests, and career aspirations. IOCS is aligned to Common Core, International Society for Technology in Education's (ISTE) National Educational Technology Standards for Students (NETS•S) and state technology curriculum standards, as well as the Partnership for 21st Century Skills Framework for 21st Century Skills. IOCS students choose from an array of OCW offerings from such schools as the Massachusetts Institute of Technology (MIT), Harvard, Yale, University of California at Berkeley, Stanford, and many others, and apply their learning to earn high school credit.

The IOCS experience is accessed through the IOCS website (sites.google.com/site/opencoursewarestudies/), which contains links to OCW offerings that are constantly updated. The site also provides an overview of the program, the IOCS Rubric, Frequently Asked Questions (FAQs), and a Google form through which students register for courses. Other documents, like periodic check-in forms, are also available on the site.

Students choose an OCW course (or part of a course) from an approved, accredited university through the IOCS website. Using the IOCS Google registration form embedded in the site, they register for their course by identifying the institution, course number, and title. Sometimes, if the course is extensive or very advanced, students may decide to complete only certain parts of that course, in which case they identify what part(s) they agree to complete at the outset. This is taken into account when they are assessed for their work.

Once they choose their OCW course, students engage in the activities provided by that particular unit of study. Learning activities vary widely from institution to institution and within disciplines, but coursework usually consists of one or more of the following: course lectures, which can be video presentations or texts; learning activities like experiments or open-ended questions; demonstrations; and interim and final assessments. Students apply themselves to these activities over the course of a high school marking period.

Students receive individualized mentoring as they progress through their OCW course. Highly motivated, gifted students who have found their "perfect" course may need little guidance, while others may benefit from varying degrees of structuring and advice along the way. IOCS mentors check in with students on a regular basis to gauge the level of mentoring intervention needed. In all cases, the advanced content and high expectations inherent in the coursework provide students with a glimpse into the demands that college poses and helps them prepare for their higher education.

Students combine their creativity with their newfound knowledge to synthesize a unique product that demonstrates and applies the new knowledge and skills they gained from the OCW. The aim is that students go beyond a static PowerPoint presentation laden with mere text and pictures and produce an actual product, whether it is the demonstration of a new skill, the creation of a physical model, the designing and conducting of an experiment, the formulation of a theory, or some other creative way to show what they've learned (see the IOCS Rubric).

The culminating IOCS experience is a five- to seven-minute student exposition of learning in front of faculty and IOCS peers. The work is assessed according to the IOCS Rubric, which is aligned to national and state standards. The rubric can be found in Appendix F. By developing a framework for the advanced learning opportunities that OCW promises, schools will enable gifted and motivated students to progress beyond the scope of their traditional secondary curriculum.

As more universities begin to make their courses available in the form of OCW and MOOC, opportunities to individualize and personalize learning will be endless. Bold leaders will view these resources as key components to district-approved independent study programs for credit. One fantastic resource for digital leaders that contains all of the necessary support structures is OCW Scholar from MIT. These courses are actually designed for independent learners who have limited additional resources available to them. The courses are substantially more complete than typical OCW courses and include custom-created content as well as materials repurposed from actual MIT classrooms. The materials are arranged in logical sequences and include multimedia such as video and simulations. OCW Scholar can be accessed at ocw .mit.edu/courses/ocw-scholar/.

What makes OCW Scholar perfect for an independent study is that everything a student, teacher, and leader needs is available here. Virtually every MIT course on this site has video lectures, assignments and solutions, recitation videos, and exams and solutions. There is also a detailed description of the course, an outline of the format, and syllabus. For the student, there is structure, a defined path, and opportunities to practice and apply what has been learned. For the teacher or independent study advisor, there are course descriptions and assessments to justify credit. For the leader, there is a legitimate means to provide a world-class learning opportunity to any student who wishes to pursue it.

SUMMARY

Digital leadership is a call to action. It is a calling to leaders to critically reflect on the learning spaces and environments that embody a school. Do they meet the needs of learners today? Do they foster and inspire creativity, provide flexible opportunities to learn, and address unique and specific interests? Are they reminiscent of what students will expect in today's world? Digital leadership drives school leaders to look past traditional constructs and incorporate trends embraced by Fortune 500 companies to transform learning spaces and environments. When energy and time are spent in this area, school will not only authentically engage students, but also better prepare them for success in today's dynamic society. The end result will be opening the door to learning while creating global scholars.

11

Discovering Opportunity

In these difficult and uncertain economic times, it is imperative that school leaders maintain and improve upon existing programs and initiatives focused on providing students with the tools for success in a digital world. Bold leadership is needed to continue to move schools forward while increasing engagement, enhancing learning, and improving student achievement. Digital leadership does not succumb to excuses imposed by the pressures of education reform or economic instability. Instead, it focuses on finding innovative solutions to deliver authentic learning experiences and support to continuously provide the best learning opportunities for students.

STRATEGIC PARTNERSHIPS

It is hard to imagine that ten years ago, parents, partnerships, and programs were running from the Maplewood Richmond Heights School District, Missouri, like it was infected with an educational virus. There was no sensible reason for outside resources to attach themselves to the district because it was failing its community in many ways. Fast forward to today, and incredible opportunities for kids are spilling from every corner of the district. This would not be possible without the resources, programming, and people power that it receives from its community, national, and global partners. Many of these initiatives were pursued and implemented as a result of the leadership of Robert Dillon, Director of Technology Integration and Information for the Affton School District, who was also the principal of Maplewood Richmond Heights Middle School.

During this journey toward becoming an interconnected district with fluid learning partnerships, a tipping point occurred when community partners were energized by the mission and core drive of the organization. This energy created a desire for more and more partners to reach out to the district, so that they could be attached to the train of innovation that was moving at a rapid clip. During this period, the staff and students of the district experienced another level of excitement, as it was now flush with new ideas and fresh ways to promote energized learning in kids. The Maplewood Richmond Heights School District was emboldened by this shift, and teachers and students leaned into the possibilities that emerged.

Throughout this period, some worried that this wave of opportunities would flood the system and blur the focus, causing mission drift. The theory was that exposing an organization to a myriad of community resources would drag the district toward the mission of the partners as opposed to the partners supporting the core work of the school. To combat this, it was essential for the school leaders at Maplewood Richmond Heights to remain steadfast to molding its portfolio of partnerships to surround its cornerstones of learning: leadership, scholarship, citizenship, and stewardship.

Another way that the Maplewood Richmond Heights School District was able to attract fresh opportunities was to craft a fresh vision that energized the community and beyond.

Partners aren't looking for schools that have a mission that slips quietly into the mix of over 90% of schools doing education. It is key for innovative school and district leaders to brand their niche, their story, their unique space in the cacophony of educational conversation. Only then will districts attract the best partners that can be sustained over time (Dillon, 2013).

Over the last ten years, Maplewood Richmond Heights School District has taken a systematic approach to building a robust set of resources and partnerships to support its students. These partnerships have included university partners, mental health partners, intraschool partners, experiential learning partners, and corporate and community partners. This vast network varies in its density of work with students, but each partnership provides time, talent, and treasured opportunities to enrich the educational experiences of the students.

In a time when interconnectedness is easier than ever to achieve, finding these partnerships has been aided by the continuous flow of resources available through social media outlets, especially through educators using Twitter to mine the vast educational landscape for ideas and possibilities. It has been amazing to watch this use of social media spread throughout the district from a few early adopters, to teacher leaders, to students. The following are some of the specific benefits that have been realized by staff and students from the opportunities and partnerships developed over the years.

University Partnerships

The Maplewood Richmond Heights partnership with Webster University allowed experts in the Reggio Emilia early childhood philosophy to be embedded in all aspects of its growth over the last decade. Partnerships with Saint Louis University, Maryville University, and Washington University in Saint Louis have brought many students to college campuses with the hopes of opening additional hearts and minds to the possibility of college success. University partnerships have also brought practicum students and adult resources into the classroom to partner with teachers in a variety of STEM (Science, Technology, Engineering, and Math) classes at the middle school and high school level. This is only a sampling of the ways that the district has found synergy with universities in supporting its students. Maplewood Richmond Heights has been careful to make sure that the partnerships are symbiotic relationships that allow both sides to benefit. This means that university classes are conducted in the schools, and a variety of classes visit district premises to experience how learning in aesthetically pleasing space supports student growth, how to integrate technology into classrooms, and how to build hope and promise in an urban school setting.

Experiential Learning Partnerships

Maplewood Richmond Heights Middle School is a school built on the metaphor of "school as expedition," which means that students are learning outside of the traditional classroom more than 20% of the school year. In order to make this possible, the need to foster and nurture partnerships was essential. Because of exceptional work by teachers and school leaders over the last decade, students in Missouri have an opportunity to learn on-site with partners at the Great Smoky Mountain Institute at Tremont in Tennessee and at the Dauphin Island Sea Lab in Alabama. These flagship partnerships are coupled to a variety of local and regional partnerships including The Audubon Center at Riverlands, Forest Park Forever, Missouri Botanical Garden, and the YMCA. Each of these experiences is designed to maximize student learning through experts in the field.

Intraschool Partnerships

Excellent schools and excellent school leaders are awakening to the fact that student achievement cannot be successfully obtained solely through competitive endeavors. Instead, schools are focusing more resources on intraschool partnerships to help them realize new levels of success for their students. This led the school leaders at Maplewood Richmond Heights to place a premium on building learning partnerships with schools throughout the country. It included a partnership with The College School in neighboring Webster Groves, Missouri. This collaboration had a fifth-grade class from The College School and eighth-grade science students from Maplewood Richmond Heights Middle School learning together about water quality, watersheds, and the sustainability of our practices surrounding water. The partnership provided students with the opportunity to build their skills of cooperation and communication. During National Novel Writing Month, one middle school teacher worked with a high school creative writing class in British Columbia, so that her students had writing mentors to support their commitment to writing every day throughout the month. Another group of middle school students are learning about the power of student voice by presenting a number of "education for sustainability" topics to audiences filled with students and staff from other schools. Teachers throughout the district have embraced their role as stewards of the entire education system, meaning that they not only support the students in their classrooms, but they also support and partner with students and classes around the world to build leaders, scholars, citizens, and stewards.

Corporate/Community Partnerships

As the drive to have students enhance their empathy for their surroundings grew, additional community and corporate partnerships were necessary for the Maplewood Richmond Heights system learning. Partners like the Dana Brown Foundation, Novus International, and the Danforth Plant Science Center were all able to provide opportunities for the students to dig more deeply into the environmental justice issues surrounding food, water, and energy. Local businesses such as Schlafly Bottleworks and Kakao Chocolate became local case studies for how companies can use the triple bottom line of people, planet, and profits to be responsible members of the community. Partners like these also allowed students to explore and learn about the social justice and economic justice issues facing individuals in the community. Funding partners like Gateway Greening, Innovative Technology Education Fund, and the Sustainable Agriculture Research and Education Program have also provided supplemental revenue streams to support the vision and mission of the district. Each of these organizations has become a perennial partner with the district, meaning the roots between the organization and the school district go beyond a single moment or a stand-alone contribution. This depth of a partnership doesn't materialize with all partnerships, and schools and districts need to be ready to be nimble in holding or folding their partnership energy, so that a majority of time can be spent tending to and growing these excellent community and corporate partnerships.

Mental Health Partnerships

In 2008, Saint Louis County voters passed a one-quartercent sales tax measure that, in turn, created a community children's service fund to provide mental health and substance abuse services for children and youths ages nineteen and under. Since this time, Maplewood Richmond Heights has built strategic partnerships with local agencies to support the students in the areas of mental and emotional health. Taking advantage of these opportunities has required a willingness to share instructional time and spaces with these organizations, and it has also required leadership to build awareness throughout the organization about the benefits that these services provide to the overall academic growth of the students. The school district has just more than half of its students living in poverty, and many other students struggle with mental health and substance abuse issues. Only through incredible agencies like Youth in Need, The National Council on Alcohol and Drug Abuse, Safe Connections, and Lutheran Family and Children's Services has the school district been able to tend to these foundational needs of the students and maintain the sustainable growth over time, leading the district to be recognized as accredited with distinction by the state of Missouri.

The future of Maplewood Richmond Heights School District remains incredibly bright, as a virtual village has been wrapped around each of the students to provide support, expert mentors, and a vision for the opportunities in life after high school. It has taken a deep commitment by school and district leaders to plant, nurture, weed, and harvest from this garden of partnerships. The beauty of planting rich soil, analyzing the nutritional needs to support the garden, and using sustainable practices surrounding partnerships is that they allow opportunities found to grow and opportunities that emerge to be realized. It is with this attitude that Maplewood Richmond Heights School District moves forward for each student that it cares for on a daily basis.

LEVERAGING SOCIAL MEDIA

The interconnectedness of the Pillars of Digital Leadership leads to continuous improvements in school culture and professional practice. As leaders begin to craft a strategy that incorporates social media and digital tools, the shifts and changes in behavior inherent in each of the six previously discussed pillars begin to take shape. Transparency through the use of social media breeds attention to programs, initiatives, and leadership style. Good news travels fast, and social media transmit the news to numerous stakeholders who are embedded in these spaces. This attention eventually leads to numerous opportunities in the form of strategic partnerships, authentic learning experiences for students, professional development, school and professional recognition, and educational technology.

There have been numerous opportunities that have come about for my school and me since embracing social media and the Pillars of Digital Leadership. After learning about the work being done at New Milford High School through social media, AverMedia donated many document cameras and digital response pens to the school in 2010. They also traveled to New Jersey from Arizona twice to train our teachers on how to use this technology. In addition to getting needed technology, NMHS teachers are now regularly using these document cameras to record their lessons, which are then uploaded to YouTube and Google Sites to assist students with their learning of the concepts.

The Edscape (edscapeconference.com) has become a strategic partnership that was formed between New Milford High School and Teq (www.teq.com), an educational technology company in the Northeast. The result of this partnership has been the formation of the Edscape Conference. This professional learning experience focusing on innovation, now in its fourth year, provides area educators with an internationally renowned keynote, sixty concurrent sessions, an innovation lab, giveaways, and meals for a fraction of the price of a traditional conference. Held on the New Milford High School campus, this event not only brings further recognition to school programs and initiatives, but provides an exceptional learning experience for all New Milford District employees free of charge.

There have also been unprecedented learning opportunities made available to our students. Connections through social media have provided New Milford High School students with some incredible learning experiences that could not be replicated in the classroom. Some examples include Skyping with *New York Times* best-selling author Daniel Pink, testing out and providing feedback on the Chromebook to engineers at the Google offices in New York City, attending a Girls Leadership Summit at the United Nations, working on a case study with the Massachusetts Institute of Technology, traveling to the Newark Museum to provide advice on how it could bring its collection into the twenty-first century with the use of Web 2.0 tools, and developing an app for the high school. All of these amazing experiences cost the district nothing and would not have been possible without the Pillars of Digital Leadership.

School and professional recognition have increased in step with our digital presence. The strategic use of social media as defined by the Pillars of Digital Leadership has resulted in national and local media coverage highlighting innovative initiatives and student accomplishments. Mainstream media outlets such as *CBS New York, USA Today, Scholastic Administrator, eSchool News,* and *Education Week* have provided consistent coverage since the evolution of the Pillars of Digital Leadership. As I have become a more transparent leader, an array of professional recognitions has followed. These include numerous national awards, acceptance to the Google Teacher Academy, and becoming an Adobe Education Leader. Prior to using social media as outlined by the Pillars of Digital Leadership, I had not one single type of recognition for the work that I was doing as a principal.

I have also had the opportunity to share my work and that of my teachers and students. Through the lens of social media, leaders make their work accessible to diverse audiences across the globe. As good ideas travel swiftly through social media channels, they will be embraced and implemented by others looking to initiate sustainable change. Over time, state and national organizations will take notice and invite digital leaders to present and showcase their work for the betterment of all.

SUMMARY

As leaders adopt and embrace the Pillars of Digital Leadership, numerous opportunities will arise in an array of areas that positively impact school culture and professional practice. By leveraging social media, leaders can share school and professional successes, build strategic partner-ships, present work to a wide array of audiences, and discover authentic learning experiences for students and staff alike. All of this can be done in a relatively cost-effective fashion while improving all facets of education. These opportunities will build a greater sense of community pride in the innova-tive work being done in education. Once understood and embraced, the Pillars of Digital Leadership will continue to work in concert with one another to bring opportunities now and in the future.

12

A Call to Action

Peter DeWitt, the principal of the Poestenkill Elementary School in Averill Park, New York, embodies digital leadership. He recently told me a story of a school leader who walked through classrooms observing some end-of-the-year activities. In one fifth-grade classroom, the students were using Glogster to make their social studies reports come alive. One student was comparing her life to that of Jacob Kohler. Another student brought in antique clothing from his great-grandmother that had been in his family for generations. In the ten minutes the school leader was in the classroom, he saw a healthy mix of real-life artifacts and the use of technology to present information.

In another classroom, a teacher flawlessly used her iPad to take pictures of student work for their portfolios. She also needed to use some of the pictures for Evernote so she could keep a record of the great work that came out of her inquiry-based plan. When the leader returned to his office, it was time for him to mix technology and real life to help a group of students. This is digital leadership in its finest form: students using real-world tools to enhance learning, with the leader modeling appropriate and effective use every step of the way.

Five fifth graders visited the school leader's office to Skype with his brother, who lives in Cairo. They had been studying Egypt for weeks and had numerous questions to ask him. After finding out the leader's brother scuba dives, the students interested in marine biology had even more questions to ask. Setting up a time to Skype with someone who actually lives in the country they were studying was a very easy process, and they all got much out of it. The students were able to learn new information, and the two brothers were able to connect.

Peter acknowledges that technology is no longer an add-on for anyone; it is a useful tool to help present, find, and collect information. Students in this school will have the skills necessary to excel in the world that is becoming more technologically advanced and dependent by the minute. By embracing the Pillars of Digital Leadership, administrators will be in a position to transform their schools in ways that will not only bring out the best in their students and teachers, but will empower key stakeholders to be involved in the process as well.

TECHNOLOGICALLY ADVANCED

Most school leaders don't feel technologically advanced. As Peter indicated, it is the norm to have several devices such as a smartphone and tablet. According to *Huffington Post Tech* (2012), "The U.N. telecom agency says there were about 6 billion subscriptions by the end of 2011—roughly one for 86 of every 100 people." That's a fairly amazing number.

Just because everyone has smartphones doesn't mean that individuals who have them are more technologically advanced than those who don't. It just means that they are connected. It's difficult these days to meet someone who does not have a cell phone or lacks a computer of some kind. Even older adults use Facebook so they can stay in touch with friends and family. Younger adults are getting away from Facebook because of the influx of parents and grandparents who are logged on. They just don't find it as cool anymore.

The *Huffington Post Tech* (2012) article goes on to say, "The Geneva-based agency says 2.3 billion people—or about one in three of the world's 7 billion inhabitants—were Internet users by the end of 2011, but there's a strong disparity between rich and developing countries."

With the influx of technology tools, and if almost everyone owns something, what does digital leadership mean? As Peter sees it, school leaders and educators certainly cannot ignore technology anymore because it has crept into every part of our lives. However, how important is it for schools to be current in technology practices? Is this even possible, considering how quickly technology changes? Is there such a thing as too much technology?

In a recent *New York Times* commentary ("How Not to Be Alone"), Jonathan Safran Foer (2013) says,

> Most of our communication technologies began as diminished substitutes for an impossible activity. We couldn't always see one another face to face, so the telephone made it possible to keep in touch at a distance. One is not always home, so the answering machine made a kind of interaction possible without the person being near his phone. Online communication originated as a substitute for telephonic communication, which was considered, for whatever reasons, too burdensome or inconvenient. And then texting, which facilitated yet faster, and more mobile, messaging. These inventions were not created to be improvements upon face-to-face communication, but a declension of acceptable, if diminished, substitutes for it.

DIGITAL LEADERSHIP

Peter acknowledges that many school leaders use their iPads or tablets to observe teachers. They may even flip their faculty meetings and parent communication from time to time, but they also need to make sure that they are teaching students and teachers how to use it properly, and when to break away from using it at all. Digital leaders may be the worst offenders because they may lack the ability to find a balance.

Foer (2013) went on to write,

> Shooting off an e-mail is easier, still, because one can hide behind the absence of vocal inflection, and of course there's no chance of accidentally catching someone. And texting is even easier, as the expectation for articulateness is further reduced, and another shell is offered to hide in. Each step "forward" has made it easier, just a little, to avoid the emotional work of being present, to convey information rather than humanity.

The job of the digital leader is not just to model the art of being connected; it's also to model the art of human conversation and unplugging the devices. Connected educators can simply say that this is a world that their students are growing up in and they are always connected, but school leaders have some responsibility to show them other aspects of the world as well.

Peter recently attended a Principal's Advisory Council meeting where a school leader had two issues to discuss with his staff. One was professional development opportunities at their faculty meetings next year and the other was a monthly breakfast. Perhaps it's just that the Principal's Advisory Council meeting took place at the end of the year, but the group was more interested in discussing the breakfast plan. Educators long for human interaction and have a need to take time to breathe and have real conversations with their colleagues. As important as technology is, and it is an important tool, so is our need to have human interaction, and digital leaders need to promote that too.

SUMMARY

Digital leadership is about transforming schools into exciting and stimulating institutions of learning where students are actively involved in applying and mastering concepts both in traditional ways and through the use of educational technology. It is a call to action for leaders at all levels to become more knowledgeable about society and look for opportunities to connect the real world to an educational system clinging to preparing students for an industrialized workforce that is no longer in need.

The Pillars of Digital Leadership provide the framework to initiate meaningful change that can ultimately transform school culture. It is up to the leader, however, to sustain these changes through establishing a clear vision, developing a strategic plan, empowering staff, creating an environment that supports risk taking, giving up a certain amount of control, modeling the effective use of educational technologies, and being the lead learner. With all of the many tools that are constantly evolving, digital leaders need to be on their toes and know where to go for support and training. One fantastic resource is the Becoming a Digital School Leader course available for free through iTunes at tinyurl.com/digital-school-leader.

Technology has the capacity to allow us to do what we do better while accomplishing the same goals. As important as technology is to digital leadership, human interaction remains the key component of changing education now and in the future. Digital leaders understand this, and when an emphasis is placed on relationship building through these interactions, as well as anticipating needed changes, the Pillars of Digital Leadership will be the guide to move from vision to reality.

Appendix A

The ISTE National Educational Technology
Standards (NETS•A) for Administrators

1. **Visionary Leadership**—Educational administrators inspire and lead development and implementation of a shared vision for comprehensive integration of technology to promote excellence and support transformation throughout the organization. Educational administrators
   a. Inspire and facilitate among all stakeholders a shared vision of purposeful change that maximizes use of digital-age resources to meet and exceed learning goals, support effective instructional practice, and maximize performance of district and school leaders
   b. Engage in an ongoing process to develop, implement, and communicate technology-infused strategic plans aligned with a shared vision
   c. Advocate on local, state, and national levels for policies, programs, and funding to support implementation of a technology-infused vision and strategic plan

2. **Digital-Age Learning Culture**—Educational administrators create, promote, and sustain a dynamic, digital-age learning culture that provides a rigorous, relevant,

and engaging education for all students. Educational administrators

a. Ensure instructional innovation focused on continuous improvement of digital-age learning

b. Model and promote the frequent and effective use of technology for learning

c. Provide learner-centered environments equipped with technology and learning resources to meet the individual, diverse needs of all learners

d. Ensure effective practice in the study of technology and its infusion across the curriculum

e. Promote and participate in local, national, and global learning communities that stimulate innovation, creativity, and digital-age collaboration

3. **Excellence in Professional Practice**—Educational administrators promote an environment of professional learning that empowers educators to enhance student learning through the infusion of contemporary technologies and digital resources. Educational administrators

a. Allocate time, resources, and access to ensure ongoing professional growth in technology fluency and integration

b. Facilitate and participate in learning communities that stimulate, nurture, and support administrators, faculty, and staff in the study and use of technology

c. Promote and model effective communication and collaboration among stakeholders using digital-age tools

d. Stay abreast of educational research and emerging trends regarding effective use of technology and encourage evaluation of new technologies for their potential to improve student learning

4. **Systemic Improvement**—Educational administrators provide digital-age leadership and management to continuously improve the organization through the effective use of information and technology resources. Educational administrators

   a. Lead purposeful change to maximize the appropriate use of technology and media-rich resources

   b. Collaborate to establish metrics, collect and analyze data, interpret results, and share findings to improve staff performance and student learning

   c. Recruit and retain highly competent personnel who use technology creatively and proficiently to advance academic and operational goals

   d. Establish and leverage strategic partnerships to support systemic improvement

   e. Establish and maintain a robust infrastructure for technology including integrated, interoperable technology systems to support management, operations, teaching, and learning

5. **Digital Citizenship**—Educational administrators model and facilitate understanding of social, ethical, and legal issues and responsibilities to an evolving digital culture. Educational administrators

   a. Ensure equitable access to appropriate digital tools and resources to meet the needs of all learners

   b. Promote, model, and establish policies for safe, legal, and ethical use of digital information and technology

   c. Promote and model responsible social interactions related to the use of technology and information

   d. Model and facilitate the development of a shared cultural understanding and involvement in global issues through the use of contemporary communication and collaboration tools

Appendix B

Twitter Memo for Parents

In an effort to increase communication with parents on the happenings at New Milford High School (NMHS), I am encouraging you to sign up to use Twitter (www.twitter.com). Twitter is a website that allows people to communicate through the exchange of quick and brief statements. I have created an account to disseminate useful information about NMHS (i.e., school news, testing, progress reports/report card dates, school events, etc.) and valuable parent resources instantaneously. The best part is, once you have signed up to "follow" the updates, you will receive these messages instantly to your Twitter page as well as your cell phone (standard text rates apply) if you have it set up.

Signing up is easy. Go to www.twitter.com, create a user profile, and once you are registered, perform a search for the school username (NewMilfordHS). Then click on the profile and select "follow."

To receive updates via text to your cell phone, you must first add your cellular device (click settings on top of the page followed by devices) and then select to turn on updates on my profile (there will then be two green check marks under my picture, one for following and one for device updates on). See below:

NewMilfordHS

✔**Following**✔ Device updates ON

You will now receive device updates via SMS for NewMilfordHS.

If you do not wish to sign up, you can still view the profile and any updates by going to the site listed below and either book marking it or adding it to your favorite places:

http://twitter.com/NewMilfordHS

http://twitter.com/NMHS_Athletics

text message updates can be shut off by clicking on settings (top right), then devices

WE ARE ON FACEBOOK AS WELL!!!! Just visit

https://www.facebook.com/NewMilfordHS and become a fan of our page!

Appendix C

Student Media Waiver

Media Permission

_____ I give permission for my child to appear in any newspaper, television show (news or any type of educational program), or through the Internet (video, blog, article) originating from the New Milford School District. The appearance could include name, photo, video, and/or resemblance. I also grant permission for New Milford High School to publish educational content created by my child (blogs, pictures, videos, etc.). It is understood that New Milford High School is not responsible for inappropriate content posted by my child or another person on any social media site that may be used in school (i.e., Flickr, YouTube, Blogs, etc.).

_____ I do not give permission for my child to appear in any newspaper, television show, or through Internet material originating from the New Milford School District.

Student Name (please print) _____

Student Signature _____ Homeroom _____

Parent/Guardian's Signature _____

Date _____

Appendix D

Professional Growth Period Model
Developed at New Milford High School

*Professional Growth Period
(Autonomy, Mastery, Purpose)*

GUIDELINES

- In response to past staff requests, noninstructional duties have again been cut down to afford you time to engage in activities related to professional growth. We will now refer to this as a Professional Growth Period (PGP).
- PGP time is to be dedicated to your becoming a better educator and learner. Depending on the semester, all teachers will have two to three duty periods off per week to engage in professional learning opportunities. Follow your passion and work to define your purpose. This time is to be spent learning, innovating, and pursuing ways to become a master educator. Think of it as a differentiated learning opportunity that caters to each of your specific needs and interests. Sample activities include:

- o Becoming a connected educator by developing and engaging in a Personal Learning Network (PLN)
    - o Researching best practices
    - o Developing innovative learning activities
    - o Creating interdisciplinary lessons
    - o Engaging in face-to-face professional development
    - o Learning to use new technologies
    - o Collaborating on projects with colleagues
- This is your time to improve your craft, build on those innovative thoughts and ideas you always wanted to pursue, and acquire new knowledge. This time is not to be used to make copies, leave the building to get coffee/food, or socialize in the faculty room.
- In order to give you the autonomy that you deserve, we will not require logs at the end-of-year conference. However, the expectation is that each staff member submits a learning portfolio at the end-of-year evaluation conference that demonstrates how PGP time was used to improve your professional practice, for example,
    - o Improve instruction
    - o Effectively integrate technology
    - o Engage students
    - o Address the Common Core Standards
    - o Increase student achievement

Please include artifacts (lesson plans, project descriptions, websites, etc.). It is entirely up to you which format you use to create your learning portfolio (e.g., binder, Google Site, etc.).

- Available resources include PD 360, Teacher Learning Community, Classroom 2.0 (www.classroom20.com), Educators PLN (edupln.com), social media tools, and various books/journals that I have in my office.
- PD 360 has a feature where you can keep a running journal of your PGP activities if you so choose. To access, click on the HOME icon on your toolbar.

PG Portfolio Log Template
**(You can use this format to help organize your portfolio.
This is optional.)**

Date:

Topic:

Activity (i.e., PD 360, Teacher Learning Community, research, webinar, innovative activity, interdisciplinary lesson, etc.):

Integration Into Practice:

Face-to-Face Training

Whether during your PGP or after school, the Administration is available by appointment to work with you on the following areas:

- Integrating Technology
  - Blogging
  - Social bookmarking (Delicious, Diigo)
  - Twitter
  - RSS Readers
  - Google+
  - Web 2.0 (Voicethread, Animoto, Padlet, Glogster, Wordle, Prezi, Poll Everywhere, Pinterest)
  - Skype
  - Productivity (Dropbox and Evernote)
  - Establishing a PLN

- Classroom management
- Cooperative learning
- Authentic learning
- Lesson design

ADDITIONAL RESOURCES

http://pinterest.com/esheninger
http://www.delicious.com/esheninger
http://www.edweb.net

Appendix E

■

Integrating Digital Tools and Content to Develop Essential Literacies

The following list of activities shows the breadth of literacies that can be developed and enhanced through the use of digital tools.

1. Make a video of a field trip or in-class activity using a digital camcorder to capture text and video. Post on TeacherTube or Vimeo as a way for students who missed the event, parents, and other teachers to experience the event/lesson. You may want to include student interviews as part of the video, asking them to reflect on the activity and on what they learned.

2. Have students view a free podcast/video (such as a video-based lesson from iTunes U) at iTunes or another website for homework. The video should be tied directly or indirectly to what you are currently studying or are about to study. Create a worksheet of viewing questions for students to complete before discussion in class. Also, challenge students to find and share additional video resources online that supplement the video you choose. You may even set up a free wiki site from PB Wiki, Wikispaces (see below), etc., for students to add their resources to a growing list.

3. Create a class blog at Edublogs, Wordpress.com, or other free blogging site you prefer. Have students use it to recap lessons, ask questions/add comments and discussion points, and post additional resources (including graphics, photos, and embedded video).

4. Create a simple text-based website using free wiki software, such as Wikispaces or PB Wiki. Students can create pages and build a great resource for test review. And in the best cases, the test review wiki can actually become part of the assessment for your class. Who contributed? What was the quality of his or her contribution?

5. Bring in a guest speaker via Skype, a free videophone service for your computer. The guest can appear in your classroom for free and can speak with your students from practically anywhere in the world! As a next step, encourage students to research and seek out their own guest speakers. In fact, you could use Skype to create a school or class-based speakers series for your students or for larger groups of participants.

6. Have students create their project work presentations and products (such as a group lab report) using collaborative creation software such as Google Docs. Google Docs allows for multiple, simultaneous edits/additions and can help group projects (especially those on a tight deadline—not that students ever procrastinate!) come together quickly, efficiently, and effectively.

7. Analyze any text passage using Wordle. Check out this presentation on 45 Interesting Ways to Use Wordle in the Classroom: http://edudemic.com/2010/07/45-interesting-ways-to-use-wordle-in-the-classroom/

8. Have students analyze paintings and comment using VoiceThread. For lesson context, see the following link where students were prompted to use this tool to build a presentation about their thoughts on the import of sugar: http://www.pbs.org/teachers/access-analyze-act-economy/curriculum/sugar-supply/imports.

Many other examples can be found here: http://ed
.voicethread.com/library/.

9. Use Twitter in the classroom to have students react to a
video clip while watching it as a group. Or students (and
the teacher!) can use Twitter as an ongoing conversation
spot during the study of an entire unit. Students can use
a hash tag (#) to group all comments into a single stream
of conversation that can be archived. Or here's a different path: For language arts classes—take short story
writing to the extreme! Challenge students to write their
autobiographies in 140 characters or less. Check out this
presentation on 30 Interesting Ways to Use Twitter in the
Classroom: http://edudemic.com/2010/07/the-
30-newest-ways-to-use-twitter-in-the-classroom/.

10. Set up a photo-sharing group on Flickr. Science students
can take pictures of environmental problems in the area
with their mobile phones and post them to the group
page. Social studies students can similarly group photos
relevant to a current local event. Art students can look
for "real-world" examples of the forms/color uses they
are studying in class. Students can comment on and discuss images as well.

11. Use cell phones for polling devices (via text) or for
answering a quiz with free software at Poll Everywhere.
More confident teachers can use this polling tool to
solicit anonymous feedback during a typical lecture ses-
sion (e.g., Does everyone understand the lecture? Are
there new areas we should be exploring as well? What
are they? Am I boring you with this lecture? What's
missing?)

12. Use Google Earth for a geography, history, cultural, and/
or biology scavenger hunt. See lessons at sitescontent
.google.com/google-earth-for-educators/Home/
google-earth-lesson-plans.

13. Have your students build a presentation on a topic of
their choice using PREZI (prezi.com).

14. Or how about creating a video using Masher (www
.masher.com), where your students can combine video
clips, audio tracks, and photos into a multimedia
montage?

Source: Adapted from PBS Teachers (www.pbs.org/teachers/digital-media-
literacy/integrating-digital-tools-and-content/).

Appendix F

Appendix F IOCS Rubric

	Outstanding (3 points)	Proficient (2 points)	Not Proficient (1 point)
Physical product	Student uses authentic tools and props to convey new knowledge acquired through specified OpenCourseWare from an approved institution of learning; this can include but is not limited to demonstrating a new skill, learning a new technology, creating a physical model, designing and conducting an experiment, and formulating a theory.	Student uses some tools or props in addition to a demonstration of knowledge acquired through specified OpenCourseWare from an approved institution of learning in the form of a traditional presentation stemming from specified OpenCourseWare from an approved institution of learning.	Student has lectured on the subject of content from OpenCourseWare from an approved institution, but no physical project is presented other than a PowerPoint, PREZI, or other digital presentation tool that contains an abundance of text but lacks depth.
Technology	Student has creatively integrated two or more technological tools and/or media resources in the construction of his or her knowledge and development of the final product.	Student has creatively integrated one technological tool or media resource in the construction of his or her knowledge and development of the final product.	Student did not integrate any technological tool or media resource in the construction of his or her knowledge and development of the final product.
Depth of learning	Exposition of learning clearly demonstrates acquisition and application of new knowledge; student is able to answer audience questions and demonstrate extended knowledge; student is likely to be able to apply learning from this project to college and career goals.	Exposition of learning demonstrates some acquisition and application of new knowledge; student may be able to answer some additional questions from audience; student may be able to apply learning from this project to college and career goals.	Exposition does not demonstrate new knowledge. OR the student shows little understanding of the knowledge or skills involved and is unlikely to be able to apply learning from this project to college and career goals.

Public speaking	Student presented original goals, as well as claims and findings; ideas were sequenced logically and with pertinent descriptions, facts, and details to accentuate main ideas; a concise summarization was provided; there was appropriate eye contact, adequate volume, and clear, correct pronunciation; student showed enthusiasm for this work.	Student presented original goals or claims and findings; ideas were presented with pertinent descriptions, facts, and details to accentuate main ideas; a summarization was provided; student attempted to provide eye contact, adequate volume, and correct pronunciation; student showed enthusiasm for this work.	Presentation lacked one or more of the following: original goals, claims/findings; pertinent descriptions, facts, details, or summarization; appropriate eye contact, adequate volume, and clear, correct pronunciation; student may not have showed enthusiasm for this work.
Studentship	All IOCS directions were followed carefully and forms filled out; all goals outlined at the outset of the project were met and completed on time; presentation was kept within time limits; all forms and feedback requirements were met. All works cited and consulted were presented in correct MLA format.	IOCS directions were generally followed carefully and all forms filled out; some but not all goals were outlined at the outset of the project; specified goals were completed on time; presentation may have been kept within time limits; most or all forms and feedback requirements were met; sources cited and consulted were presented.	One or more of the following is evident: • IOCS directions/forms not carefully followed/filled out • Goals not outlined at the outset of the project and may not have been completed on time • Presentation not kept within time limits • Forms/feedback requirements not met • Works cited and consulted not presented
Score			

(Continued)

Appendix F   Continued

Total project score _____   Grade[1] _____

Comments _____

_____

_____

_____

_____

_____

_____

_____

_____

_____

References

Alexander, B. (2008). Web 2.0 and emergent multiliteracies. *Theory Into Practice, 47,* 150–160.

Anderson, S., & Stiegelbauer, S. (1994). Institutionalization and renewal in a restructured school. *School Organization, 14*(3), 279–293.

Arnold, M., Perry, R., Watson, R., Minatra, K., & Schwartz, R. (2006). The practitioner: How successful principals lead and influence. Ypsilanti, MI: National Council of Professors of Educational Administration. Retrieved February 16, 2013, from http://cnx.org/content/m14255/1.1

Barseghian, T. (2011). Straight from the DOE: Dispelling myths about blocked sites. *Mindshift: How we will learn.* Retrieved December 26, 2012, from http://blogs.kqed.org/mindshift/2011/04/straight-from-the-doe-facts-about-blocking-sites-in-schools/

Bloomberg. (2012). Average household has 5 connected devices, while some have 15-plus. Retrieved December 23, 2012, from http://go.bloomberg.com/tech-blog/2012-08-29-average-household-has-5-connected-devices-while-some-have-15-plus/

Bouffard, S. (2008). Tapping into technology: The role of the Internet in family–school communication. Retrieved September 21, 2013, from http://www.hfrp.org/publications-resources/browse-our-publications/tapping-into-technology-the-role-of-the-internet-in-family-school-communication

Britten, D. (2013). Personal interview.

Carter, D. (2013). Personal interview.

Carver, J. (2013). Personal interview.

Casero-Ripollés, A. (2012). Beyond newspapers: News consumption among young people in the digital era. *Comunicar, 20*(39).

Childwise. (2012). Trends in media use. UK Council for Child Internet Safety. Retrieved December 23, 2012, from http://

www.saferinternet.org.uk/Content/Childnet/Safer-Internet-Centre/downloads/Research_Highlights/UKCCIS_RH_28_Childwise.pdf

Churches, A. (2008). 21st century pedagogy. Retrieved July 1, 2013, from http://edorigami.wikispaces.com/21st+Century+Pedagogy

Cook, S. (2013). Personal interview.

Couros, A. (2006). Examining the open movement: Possibilities and implications for education. Retrieved from http://www.scribd .com/doc/3363/Dissertation-Couros-FINAL-06-WebVersion

Couros, G. (2013). Personal interview.

Davies, D., Henderson, A. T., Johnson, V., & Mapp, K. L. (2006). *Beyond the bake sale: The essential guide to family-school partnerships.* New York, NY: The New Press.

Demsky, J. (2012). 7 habits of highly effective tech-leading principals. *THE Journal.* Retrieved December 29, 2012, from http://thejournal.com/articles/2012/06/07/7-habits-of-highly-effective-tech-leading-principals.aspx

Dewan, S. (2012). To stay relevant in a career, workers train nonstop. *New York Times.* Retrieved September 13, 2013 from http://www .nytimes.com/2012/09/22/business/to-stay-relevant-in-a-career-workers-train-nonstop.html?pagewanted=all

Dillon, R. (2013). Personal interview.

DuFour, R., DuFour, R., & Eaker, R. (2008). *Revisiting professional learning communities at work: New insights for improving schools.* Bloomington, IN: Solution Tree.

Education Week. (2011). Technology in education. Retrieved December 23, 2012, from http://www.edweek.org/ew/issues/technology-in-education/

Edudemic. (2012). Pedagogical framework for digital tools. Retrieved March 23, 2013, from http://edudemic .com/2012/12/a-pedagogical-framework-for-digital-tools/

Edutopia. (2012). *What works in education.* The George Lucas Educational Foundation. Retrieved December 23, 2012, from http://www.edutopia.org

Epstein, J. L. (2011). School, family, and community partnerships: *Preparing educators and improving schools* (2nd ed.). Philadelphia, PA: Westview Press.

Federal Communications Commission. (2011). Child Internet Protection Act. Retrieved September 14, 2013, from http:// www.fcc.gov/guides/childrens-internet-protection-act

Ferriter, W. M. (2013). Technology is a tool, not a learning outcome. Retrieved July 13, 2013, from http://blog

.williamferriter.com/2013/07/11/technology-is-a-tool-not-a-learning-outcome/

Ferriter, W. M., Ramsden, J. T., & Sheninger, E. C. (2011). *Communicating & connecting with social media*. Bloomington, IN: Solution Tree.

Finette, P. (2012, November 1). The participation culture: Pascal Finette at TEDxorangecoast. Retrieved January 5, 2013, from http://www.youtube.com/watch?v=yJMnVieDfD0

Foer, J. S. (2013). How not to be alone. *New York Times*. Retrieved June 27, 2013, from http://www.nytimes .com/2013/06/09/opinion/sunday/how-not-to-be-alone .html?pagewanted=all&src=ISMR_AP_LO_MST_FB&_r=0

Friedman, T. (2005). *The world is flat*. New York, NY: Farrar, Straus and Giroux

Fullan, M. (2001). *Leading in a culture of change*. San Francisco, CA: Jossey-Bass.

Fullan, M. (2008). *The six secrets of change* San Francisco, CA: Jossey-Bass.

Gee, J. P. (2007). *What video games have to teach us about learning and literacy* (2nd ed.). New York, NY: Macmillan.

Gerstein, J. (2013). *Schools are doing Education 1.0; talking about doing Education 2.0; when they should be planning Education 3.0*. User Generated Education. Retrieved March 23, 2013, from http:// usergeneratededucation.wordpress.com/2013/03/22/schools-are-doing-education-1–0-talking-about-doing-education-2–0-when-they-should-be-planning-education-3–0/

Gladwell, M. (2008). *Outliers*. New York, NY: Little, Brown and Company.

Glazer, N. (2009). Outliers, by Malcolm Gladwell. *Education Next*. Retrieved December 29, 2012, from http://educationnext.org/ nature-or-culture/

Godin, S. (2010). *Linchpin: Are you indispensible?* New York, NY: Penguin Group.

Gordon, D. (2010). Wow! 3D content awakens the classroom. *THE Journal*. Retrieved December 26, 2012, from http://thejournal .com/articles/2010/10/01/wow-3d-content-awakens-the-classroom.aspx

Gronn, P. (2000). Distributed properties: A new architecture for leadership. *Educational Management and Administration, 28*(3), 371.

Harris, A., & Lambert, L. (2003). *Building leadership capacity for school improvement*. Maidenhead, UK: Open University Press.

Haystead, M., & Marzano, R. (2009). Evaluation study of the effects of Promethean ActivClassroom on student achievement.

Retrieved December 26, 2012, from http://www1.promethean-world.com/server.php?show=nav.19203

Herold, D., & Fedor, D. (2008). *Change the way you lead change.* Stanford, CA: Stanford University Press.

Hilt, L. (2013). Personal interview.

Hopkins, D., & Jackson, D. (2003). Building the capacity for leading and learning. In A. Harris, C. Day, M. Hadfield, D. Hopkins, A. Hargreaves, & C. Chapman (Eds.), *Effective leadership for school improvement* (pp. 84–105). London, UK: Routledge Falmer.

Hoyle, J. R., English, F. W., & Steffy, B. E. (1998). *Skills for successful 21st century school leaders: Standards for peak performers.* Arlington, VA: American Association of School Administrators.

Huffington Post Tech. (2012). World has about 6 billion cell phone subscribers, according to U.N. telecom agency report. Retrieved June 27, 2013, from http://www.huffingtonpost.com/2012/10/11/cell-phones-world-subscribers-six-billion_n_1957173.html

International Society for Technology in Education. (2009). *National educational technology standards.* Retrieved January 5, 2013, from http://www.iste.org/standards/nets-for-administrators

Jacobs, R. (2009). Leveraging the "networked" teacher: The Professional Networked Learning Collaborative. Retrieved February 24, 2013, from http://educationinnovation.typepad.com/my_weblog/2009/06/leveraging-the-networked-teacher-the-professional-networked-learning-collaborative.html

Johnson, S. (2006). *Everything bad is good for you.* New York, NY: Riverhead.

Jones, R. (2008). *Leading change in high schools.* Rexford, NY: International Center for Leadership in Education.

Jukes, I., McCain, T., & Crockett, L. (2010). *Understanding the digital generation: Teaching and learning in the new digital landscape.* Kelowna, Canada: 21st Century Fluency Project [copublished with Corwin].

Kelly, F. S., McCain, T., & Jukes, I. (2009). *Teaching the digital generation: No more cookie-cutter high schools.* Thousand Oaks, CA: Corwin.

Killion, J. (2013). *Meet the promise of content standards: Tapping technology to enhance professional learning.* Oxford, OH: Learning Forward.

Kouzes, J. M., & Posner, B. Z. (2007). *The leadership challenge* (4th ed.). San Francisco, CA: Jossey-Bass.

Larkin, P. (2013). Personal interview.

LeLoup, J. W., & Ponterio, R. (2000). *Enhancing authentic language learning experiences through Internet technology.* Report No.

EDO-FL-00–02. Washington, DC: Office of Educational Research and Improvement.

Lemke, C. (2008). *Multimodal learning through media: What the research Says.* San Jose, CA: Cisco Systems, Inc.

Lemke, C., Coughlin, E., Garcia, L., Reifsneider, D., & Bass, J. (2009). *Leadership for Web 2.0 in education: Promise and reality.* Culver City, CA: Metri Group. Commissioned by CoSN through support from the John D. and Catherine T. MacArthur Foundation.

Lemke, C., Coughlin, E., & Reifsneider, D. (2009). *Technology in schools: What the research says: An update.* Culver City, CA: Commissioned by Cisco.

Lipani, M. C. (2008). An encounter of the third kind. In L. Corroy (Ed.), *Youth and Media* (pp. 13–36). Paris, France: Vuibert.

Livingstone, S. (2008). Taking risky opportunities in youthful content creation: Teenagers' use of social networking sites for intimacy, privacy and self-expression. *New Media Society, 10*(3), 393–411.

Mediratta, B. (2007). The Google way: Give engineers room. *New York Times.* Retrieved April 6, 2013, from http://www .nytimes.com/2007/10/21/jobs/21pre.html?_r=3&

Mielke, D. (1999). *Effective teaching in distance education.* Report No. EDO-SP-1999–5. Washington, DC: Office of Educational Research and Improvement.

mobiThinking. (2012). Global mobile statistics 2012 home: All the latest stats on mobile Web, apps, marketing, advertising, subscribers, and trends. Retrieved December 23, 2012, from http:// mobithinking.com/mobile-marketing-tools/latest-mobile-stats

Moran, P. (2013). Personal interview.

National Association of Secondary School Principals. (2011). *Breaking ranks: The comprehensive framework for school improvement.* Reston, VA: Author.

National Research Council. (2012). *Education for life and work: Developing transferable knowledge and skills in the 21st century.* Washington, DC: The National Academies Press.

Newcomb, A. (2003). Peter Senge on organizational learning. *The School Administrator.* Alexandria, VA: American Association of School Administrators. Retrieved from http://www.aasa.org/ SchoolAdministratorArticle.aspx?id=9192

Niels, J. (2012). A pedagogical framework for digital tools. Retrieved from http://www.edudemic.com/a-pedagogical-framework-for-digital-tools/

Olins, W. (2008). *The brand handbook.* London, UK: Thames & Hudson.

Peters, T. (1999). *The brand you 50.* New York, NY: Knopf.

Pew Internet and American Life Project. (2007). *Social networking websites and teens, 2006.* Washington, DC: Author. Retrieved December 23, 2012, from http://www.pewinternet.org/Reports/2007/Social-Networking-Websites-and-Teens.aspx

Pew Internet and American Life Project. (2009). *Adults on social networks, 2005–2009.* Washington, DC: Author. Retrieved December 23, 2012, from http://www.pewinternet.org/Reports/2009/Adults-and-Social-Network-Websites.aspx

Pew Internet and American Life Project. (2010). *Social media and young adults.* Washington DC: Author. Retrieved December 23, 2012 from http://www.pewinternet.org/Reports/2010/Social-Media-and-Young-Adults.aspx

Pew Internet and American Life Project. (2011). *Social networking sites and our lives.* Washington, DC: Author. Retrieved December 23, 2013 from http://www.pewinternet.org/~/media/Files/Reports/2011/PIP%20-%20Social%20networking%20sites%20and%200ur%20lives.pdf

Pink, D. (2011). *Drive: The surprising truth on what motivates us.* New York, NY: Riverhead.

Prensky, M. (2001). Digital natives, digital immigrants. *On the Horizon, 9*(5).

Riedel, C. (2012, February 1). Digital learning: What kids really want. Retrieved January 5, 2013, from http://thejournal.com/articles/2012/02/01/digital-learning-what-kids-really-want.aspx

Rodriguez, N. (2010, July 26). Exactly how much are the times a-changin'? *Newsweek,* p. 56.

Rosen, D., & Nelson, C. (2008). Web 2.0: A new generation of learners and education. *Computers in the Schools, 25*(3), 211–225.

Rubin, P. (2013). Personal interview.

Rule, A. (2006). The components of authentic learning. *Journal of Authentic Learning, 3*(1), 1–10.

Schrum, L., & Levin, B. (2009). *Leading 21st century schools.* Thousand Oaks, CA: Corwin.

Skiba, D. J., & Baron, A. J. (2006). Adapting your teaching to accommodate the net generation of learners. *Online Journal of Issues in Nursing, 11*(2).

Simmons, B. (2010, March 5). Leadership 3.0 [Web log post]. Retrieved December 22, 2012, from http://www.bretlsimmons.com/2010–03/leadership-3–0/

Spivack, N. (n.d.). Web 3.0: The third generation web is coming. Retrieved from http://lifeboat.com/ex/web.3.0

Stager, G. (2005). The high cost of incrementalism in educational technology implementation. Retrieved July 6, 2013, from

https://docs.google.com/viewer?url=http%3A%2F%2Fstager
.org%2Farticles%2Fincrementalism.pdf

Stepien, W., & Gallagher, S. (1993). Problem-based learning: As authentic as it gets. *Educational Leadership, 50*(7), 25–28.

Strategy Analytics. (2012). A quarter of households worldwide now have wireless home networks. Retrieved December 23, 2012, from http://www.strategyanalytics.com/default.aspx?mod =pressreleaseviewer&a0=5193

Tomlinson, C. (2011). Respecting students. *Educational Leadership, 69*(1), 94–95.

U.S. Department of Education. (2012). *Evidence framework: Expanding evidence approaches for learning in a digital world.* Retrieved December 30, 2012, from http://www.ed.gov/edblogs/technology/evidence-framework/

Vest, C. M. (2004). Why MIT decided to give away all its course materials via the Internet. *The Chronicle of Higher Education, 50*(21).

Web 2.0. (2013). In *Wikipedia.* Retrieved September 11, 2013, from http://en.wikipedia.org/wiki/Web_2.0

Whitaker, T. (2003). *What great principals do differently: Fifteen things that matter the most.* Larchmount, NY: Eye on Education.

Whitehurst, G. J. (2009). Don't forget curriculum. Washington, DC: Brookings. Retrieved February 16, 2013, from www.brookings .edu/papers/2009/1014_curriculum_whitehurst.aspx

Zhao, Y. (2012). *World class learners.* Thousand Oaks, CA: Corwin.

Index

221

CORWIN

A SAGE Company

The Corwin logo—a raven striding across an open book—represents the union of courage and learning. Corwin is committed to improving education for all learners by publishing books and other professional development resources for those serving the field of PreK–12 education. By providing practical, hands-on materials, Corwin continues to carry out the promise of its motto: **"Helping Educators Do Their Work Better."**

The Ontario Principals' Council (OPC) is a voluntary association for principals and vice-principals in Ontario's public school system. We believe that exemplary leadership results in outstanding schools and improved student achievement. To this end, we foster quality leadership through world-class professional services and supports. As an ISO 9001 registered organization, we are committed to **"quality leadership—our principal product."**

Praise for *Digital Leadership*

Digital Leadership *is a great one-stop shopping place to learn about all the key ingredients you will need for success in the digital age. Sheninger connects the dots with his seven pillars, his listing of obstacles and ways to overcome them, and the integrated solution that brings it all together. Comprehensive, clear, practical—get it and use it today!*

> Michael Fullan, Author, *Motion Leadership*, Dean and Professor Emeritus
> Ontario Institute for Studies in Education
> Toronto, Canada

Digital Leadership *is essential reading for any education leader trying to figure out how technology can strengthen schools—and what pitfalls to avoid. Eric Sheninger masterfully makes the connections as to how technology can strengthen schools, providing an essential guide for today's leaders in education. This is a readable, practical book!*

> Cindy Johanson, Executive Director, Edutopia
> The George Lucas Educational Foundation
> San Rafael, CA

Eric recognizes that ongoing professional development is the key to helping staff meet the challenges of the future. He shares how to leverage technology to build a strong, school-based professional learning agenda when other resources are not meeting the needs of your faculty and students. His story and tools will be inspirational to others.

> Stephanie Hirsh, Executive Director
> Learning Forward
> Dallas, TX

Digital Leadership *is a focused guide to using the many new channels of modern communication to engage families, tell your school's story, inspire staff growth and connection, and bring new relevance to the classroom. If you're feeling overwhelmed by all the options out there, this book will give you a head start on mastering your social media strategy.*

> Daniel H. Pink, Author, *To Sell Is Human*
> Washington, DC

This book is THE book on digital leadership. There is no one I can recommend more highly than the most connected educational leader today—Eric Sheninger—to help us navigate all of the changes taking place in classrooms, schools and districts. The book is perfect to help everyone initiate transformational change in a digital world. Whether you are a cutting-edge techie or a nervous newbie, this book is for you.

> Todd Whitaker, Ph.D., Professor of Educational Leadership
> Indiana State University
> Terre Haute, IN

Eric has created a must-read book for principals seeking to bring their schools into the digital age. He has created the compelling case for the many ways digital tools can have a powerful, positive effect in our schools. From classroom practice to the way in which we create the digital footprint of our schools, Eric steps us through how school leaders can evolve to meet the challenges of our modern age.

Chris Lehmann, Founding Principal
Science Leadership Academy
Philadelphia, PA

Eric Sheninger's new book is a red-hot, relevant guide to navigating the technology-driven, tectonic shifts taking place in education today. While education leaders of all stripes are groping for answers as the ground beneath them shifts, Digital Leadership *provides a reliable, practical, and tested road map for leading in the digital age.*

Errol St. Clair Smith, Executive Director
Academy of Education Arts and Sciences
Glendale, CA

There are books on technology that don't show you how to change. There are books on how to change that have nothing to say about technology. Then there are curmudgeonly commentaries that are dismissive about change and technology in equal measure. Eric Sheninger's book alters all that. Through personal testimony, practical examples, and a commitment to clear professional learning, Digital Leadership *opens your mind and shows you the tools that will make you think again about what twenty-first-century learning can really look like. If your iPads are used as notebooks, your SMART Boards are glorified whiteboards, and your school has an electronic ban on access to everything, this book will make you look at technology and learning with totally different eyes.*

Professor Andy Hargreaves, BA, PhD, Hon Doc (Uppsala), FRSA
Thomas More Brennan Chair in Education
Lynch School of Education, Boston College
Chestnut Hill, MA

Digital Leadership *is a must-read for every school leader. Filled with inspiring stories of transformation from real, practicing campus leaders, along with an appendix filled with resources anyone can take to campus and use today, Eric Sheninger's work is certain to be one of the most valuable resources in your professional library.*

Carrie Jackson, Principal
Timberview Middle School
Fort Worth, TX

Eric Sheninger's book builds upon his impressive accomplishments as a digital leader. I have had a chance to learn from Eric through his involvement with Digital Learning Day, and I am thrilled that others can learn even more from him about leading schools to maximize the potential of digital learning and asking the tough questions to more effectively meet the needs of each student. Eric's bold approach to school reform and the thoughtful pillars he lays out in this book provide important guidance for other education leaders striving to implement digital learning.

Bob Wise, President
Alliance for Excellent Education
Former Governor of West Virginia

"Digital leadership" is more than a catchphrase—it's how school principals must lead students, parents, and teachers—and no one is better equipped to describe this leadership approach than Eric Sheninger.

Digital Leadership is a carefully crafted and highly readable book that simultaneously provides a view of digital leadership from 60,000 feet alongside a boots-on-the-ground realist's view of modern schooling. From setting aside fears of technology to understanding the importance of communication, public relations, and even branding, Digital Leadership offers compelling recommendations not only focused on the need to change but also on best ways to sustain change.

It's possible that Eric saved the best for last when he put into words the concept of the networked teacher and how students must be engaged in new and exciting ways, for, truly, school leadership has always been about helping teachers engage students.

Finally, don't mistake this as a book on technology. From the first to the last page, Eric's book is all about school leadership, one that I highly recommend to every school leader.

William Bushaw, Executive Director
PDK International
Arlington, VA

I loved this book! It is filled with many examples of how technology is impacting learning in classrooms across the country. Whether you are a technology guru or learning to embrace technology, every school administrator should read this book to learn ways to prepare their students to be successful in the twenty-first century. Leadership 3.0 is a mindset that every school administrator needs to embrace and lead with. I am going to request that my superintendent purchase it for my fellow administrators, along with the educators on our district technology team.

Jessica Johnson, Principal and District Assessment Coordinator
Dodgeland Elementary School
Juneau, WI

What a great read! Digital Leadership situates the trends in technology and education within a historical context and provides a blueprint to the reader for a navigable pathway for the future. And it manages to do so in a way that is empowering and energizing, while still addressing the very real fears and challenges facing any leader standing at this nexus of authentic educational reform. It is a very rare blend of philosophy, pedagogy, and practical, roll-up-your-sleeves how tos.

Natalie Bernasconi, La Paz Middle School NBCT Teacher
Technology Literacy Coach
University of California, Santa Cruz Lecturer
Google Certified Teacher
Salinas, CA

I can't wait to get real copies of this in the hands of teacher leaders and colleagues. I absolutely believe that this work has the potential for tremendous impact. We have waited too long for this book, and the time is ripe to move forward with the information it has to offer. I look forward to book studies and networking with my colleagues about how they have successfully employed these ideas and strategies.

David G. Daniels, Principal
Susquehanna Valley Senior High School
Conklin, NY

How do school leaders transform themselves from the leadership style of today to become digital leaders of tomorrow? Eric Sheninger's Digital Leadership *is an easy read for those who want to begin the transition to digital leadership but have been afraid to take the first step. More than merely a "how to" book,* Digital Leadership *is a clarion call to action that compels the reader to do something now to transform schools into "vibrant learning communities that are connected and allow social media to unleash creativity in learners."*

Digital Leadership *addresses the growing disconnect between the world our students inhabit and the world in which they are educated. Replete with stories and concrete examples of "how to,"* Digital Leadership *is a must-read for any school leader who recognizes that we stand at a crossroads in education where innovative leaders who possess the courage, passion, knowledge, and skills believe that "technology is not just a shiny tool that can increase engagement but a conduit to endless possibilities that can enhance every facet of what we do in education." A must-read.*

JoAnn Bartoletti
Executive Director
National Association of Secondary School Principals
Reston, VA